Transforming Society

Transforming
Society

Copyright © Brett Johnson
All rights reserved. No part of this book may be reproduced or transmitted in any form or by any means, electronic or mechanical, including photocopying, recording, or by any information storage and retrieval system, without permission in writing from the Publisher. All quoted scriptures are from the New International Version (NIV) of the Holy Bible unless stated in the text.

Trademarks and Copyrights
The following are registered trademarks of The Institute for Innovation, Integration & Impact, Inc.:

> Repurposing Business—Transforming Society® and **rēp**
> The head of a think tank, hands of a business, heart of philanthropy.®
> Partnering with leaders to maximize Impact®
> The 10-P Model®
> The 10-F Model®

Published by

Indaba Publishing, *a division of*

The Institute for Innovation, Integration & Impact, Inc.®
www.inst.net
+1.866.9INDABA

ISBN: 978-0-9826962-4-8
All rights reserved.

Book Cover and Graphic Design by Huey Nguyen.

Contact Information:
1-866-9INDABA
info@inst.net

Dedication

To my daughter,
Fay Maree,
a world changer

Table of Contents

Transforming Society Snapshot	8-9
Endorsements	11
Acknowledgements	13
Preface	15
Synopsis	17

Part 1—Spheres of Society 21

History has a way of repeating itself 23
James Orr 24
Abraham Kuijper 25
Dr. Francis Schaeffer 25
Bill Bright and Loren Cunningham 26
Today 28
Good facets of mountain thinking 29
Detractors 31
The road between dominionism and defeatism 34
Domainationalism 35
Scriptures covering The Mountain of the Lord 36
Top-down theology 39
A place of perspective 39
What happens on the Mountain of the Lord 40
The scary "-isms" 45
The three missing spheres 48
The 10 molehills explained 53
How does one delineate a sphere, mountain, or molehill? 54
Where does the church fit into this? 55
Scrapping "Business as Missions" 56
Spheres are launching pads not life sentences 58
If you have to keep changing hats 58

Part 2—Assets of Society 61

Distinguish spheres from assets 63
Nehemiah's Public Private Partnership 65

Part 3—Foundations of Societies 73

Foundations of a City 75
The dark side and sunny side of the molehills 76
Operating Model 76
Key Performance Indicators 77
Strongmen, Giants 77
Glory 78
Keys to Reconciliation, Alignment 79

Part 4—Competencies Required to Transform Society 91

Created for unity, marked by division..93
We prefer to work alone 93
The work of transformation is bigger than any of us..................94
It takes a network 94
Households are the keyhole to all sectors 96
BELTS 99
Societies are relational 101
Business must be defined afresh..102
Transforming Society requires repurposing spheres 105
Dislodged by difficulty 107
Impact at the intersection of spheres...108
Called Corporations 108
Repurposing Business 110

Part 5—The Glory of God 113

How we come down the Mountain of the Lord 115
The results of the Mountain of the Lord......................................117
Nations transformed 118
The Glory of God made practical..118
The Glory of God in an organization 132
Purpose...133
Product 133
Positioning 133
Presence 133
Partnering 133
Process 134
People 134
Planning...134
Place...135
Profit 135
The Glory of God in an individual 136
Family...136
Fun 136
Fitness 136
Feelings..136
Faith 137

Friendships 137
Fulfillment at Work...137
Function in Society..138
Fresh Thinking...138
Finances 138
Glory stories from **rēp** Ventures 139

Part 6—Phases of Nationhood 143

Phases of development 145
The cycle can be broken...148
Where does the Church fit into this? 149
Micro-ordering can have unintended outcomes 153

Part 7—Call to Action 157

Things I think we agree on..159
Come and let us go..160
From Mountain to Molehills...161
Prepare the way 162
Transforming Society 164

Appendices 169

Transformational Tools 171

Repurposing Business 171
Kingdom Business Assessment 171
Kingdom Impact Assessment...171
Societal Impact Assessment..171
Asset Evaluation...172
Public Private Partnerships 173
PPP Examples...174

Index 175

About the Author 179

Other Books by the Author 181

Transforming Society

NEED

SOCIETY NEEDS FIXING

COM-MISSION

DISCIPLES OF JESUS CHRIST HAVE BEEN GIVEN A GLOBAL MANDATE

THREE EXTREME RESPONSES

DEFEATISTS
We cannot make disciples of nations

DOMINIONISTS
Establish God's "Government" NOW

EVANGELISTS
Get a critical mass of people "saved"

A GROWING CONSENSUS

SOCIETY CAN BE TRANSFORMED

KEY ELEMENTS

BUILDING ASSETs

REPURPOSING SPHERES

TRANSFORMING SOCIETY

RELAYING FOUNDATIONs

RESTORING GLORY

TOOLS

A NETWORK OF TRANSFORMED COMPETENCIES

ASSESSMENTS OF REALITY

PRACTICAL PLANS & MEASUREMENTS

SIGNS & WONDERS FOLLOWING

BENEFITS

GROWTH OF INFLUENCE OF CHRIST

IMPROVED HUMAN CONDITION

RIGHTEOUS LEADERSHIP & GOVERNANCE

Transforming Society

Many things have improved over the centuries, but many societal ills remain: poverty, illiteracy, slavery, oppression, illness, idolatry, greed, etc.

NEED

Jesus Christ said, "Go into all the world and make disciples of all nations, teaching them to obey everything I have commanded you."

COM-MISSION

Some believe it is impossible to influence whole people-groups to become followers of the person or ways of Jesus. Others believe, "if we get enough people making professions of faith, society will change"; a final camp believes "Christians" should head institutions today.

THREE EXTREME RESPONSES

There is a growing consensus that the biblical mandate is both possible and urgent: all things (cosmos) must be reconciled to truth. This goes well beyond the message of "salvation" to include reformation. Society can be transformed.

A GROWING CONSENSUS

Exercising a "ministry of reconciliation" requires competencies of the Spirit: Relaying ancient foundations, building the infrastructure and assets of society, repurposing every sphere, and restoring the glory of God to all of life.

KEY ELEMENTS

No group can do the job alone. It is a collaborative effort requiring a breadth of competencies, or a network of transformational capabilities. Another much-needed toolset is assessments to understand the before and after reality. Practical plans, in various forms, are essential to take us beyond wishful thinking. Finally, the efforts of man have to be matched, step by step, with the miracles of God if transformation is to happen.

TOOLS

God loves the world so He wants it fixed. There are a number of ways the benefit of "the increase of His government and peace" are manifest. He is unlimited: imagining restored glory is our privilege in partnering with Him.

BENEFITS

When I gave my life to Christ I gave it all—I gave myself, my family and my business. God's plan is to renew every part of life; moreover God deserves to be glorified in every sphere of life. Brett Johnson's Transforming Society is an incredible tool that will help you to honour Christ with everything you are and all you have. It is filled with Godly revelation, balanced with substantial research, and capped-off with practical and useful tools and insights. I highly recommend it!

—*Graham Power*
Chairman of the Power Group of Companies. Founder of the Global Day of Prayer and Unashamedly Ethical movements. Author of 'Not by might nor by Power—the account of the Global Day of Prayer'

Transforming Society is a "must read soon" for all church leaders. This book articulates where the Church should be at in early 21st century.

—*Iain Muir*
International Director, Youth With a Mission, Switzerland

Endorsements

Brett's ability to be both practical and pursue the supernatural intervention of heaven are both evident in this book. None of us can be content with just attending church. Brett once again gives us tools to step outside the church and pursue a transformed society.

—Paul Manwaring
Overseer, Global Legacy, Bethel Church, Redding, California

Transforming Society is an owner's manual to seeing nations fulfill their destiny. It is rare to find a book that imparts great faith and substantial tools to see cities and nations do more and become more. Heaven is very excited about this book and so are we!

—Anne Kalvestrand
Overseer, International Transformation Training, Bethel
Director, The Art of Peace Institute

Some years ago I worked for 12 months in two poor townships in the Eastern Cape of South Africa and I saw the need for transformation of societies through all the different community spheres. After reading Brett's book, Transforming Society, I can recommend this as one of the first books that effectively identifies and addresses the makeup of society and the role each of us can play in building God's Kingdom though our spheres. Congratulations, Brett—what an amazing book!

—Gerhardt Jooste
Group CEO, Prosperito

*E*ffective ministry requires a sound theology matched with an effective strategy. I found both of these in Transforming Society: A framework for fixing a broken world. Brett Johnson has captured the biblical theology of work, worship and worth in a sound and creative manner in the pages of this book. His insights reflect a wealth of practical experience and a depth of theological insight. I recommend this book to both theologians and practitioners of Christian ministry.

—*Dr. Dion Forster*
Chaplain to the Power Group of Companies,
Research Fellow in Theology at the University of Stellenbosch
Co-author of 'Transform your work life: Turn your ordinary
day into an extraordinary calling'

*B*rett Johnson invites us to think practically and principally about the Kingdom on earth as it is in heaven, in multiple spheres. We are invited to take Jesus seriously, the fact that he reigns over all things and what his transforming power might mean for a transformed society that offers hints at the future even now.

—*Dr. Cherith Nordling*
Professor / Author / Theologian

Acknowledgements

Solomon said that there is nothing new under the sun. What I am writing about in this book has some nuggets, to be sure, but it builds on the work of others. I would therefore like to begin by acknowledging the thinking of countless people who have gone before. People like Abraham Kuijper, Bill Bright, Loren Cunningham, Landa Cope and Alistair Petrie have been thinking about these topics for a long time. They are not alone, as we shall see. Today there is a new group of sphere evangelists and the language has shifted from domains, or spheres, to mountains. I cannot list all of them, because I would inevitably leave out key thinkers and practitioners, but I simply want to acknowledge that many have thought long and hard about the components of society.

A special word of thanks goes, however, to my friend Seelok Ting. When See and Ophelia came to visit Lyn and me in February 2009 he was on his way back from a "seven mountains" conference. He told me with concern, "No one was talking about the mountain of the Lord." He shared some of his passion for the topic and I chatted about my perspectives on the advantages and shortages of present mountain thinking.

I originally started this book as a booklet on *The Mountain of the Lord,* but my friend Iain Muir rightly pointed out that it has a wider scope and call. So it has evolved to what you have in your hands: a framework for transforming society based upon a biblical worldview. It is brief, of course, so it sketches in pen and ink that which requires much color to bloom—I trust that it will stimulate you to add the pallete of your own life as you team with us in Transforming Society.

14   Transforming Society

Preface

Years ago I was asked to speak at a leadership school for career missionaries. As a businessman I seemed to be an unusual choice. The Chancellor of the university was a good friend of mine and an integrated thinker. He had recommended to the school leader that we come and speak about leadership and how organizations actually work. The school leader was less convinced. In fact, when he introduced me and the team from The Institute he said, "If you want to know why we have six businesspeople speaking to us for a week, ask God!" He himself had little clue.

The first presentation I made was titled "Where do we get our authority from?" I knew that the gathered leaders understood the seven mind molders, and they were well versed in thinking about the domains of influence in society. I also perceived, however, that they had interpreted Abraham Kuijper's "sphere sovereignty" with a few twists:

- They believed "missions" was a sphere.

- They knew I was not a traditional missionary, but, in their view, I was merely a businessman. (That fact that I also ran a mission organization and had pastored a church was less relevant because I was not from their specific tribe.)

- They believed I had authority in the realm of business.

- But they did not really believe that a businessman had authority in the "domain" of missions.

I therefore had to start the week tackling this different, but just as deadly, expression of dichotomy. I did so by postulating that Wisdom personified in the book of Proverbs had a seat above the spheres or domains. As kingdom people, our authority transcends mountains. In fact, things we see as "the seven mountains" are at best molehills. In this book I will unpack the benefits and dangers of present thinking about the so-called mountains of society.

Before you push this book aside because some of your favorite leaders have endorsed "the seven mountains" I want to state that 7Mountain thinking can be very helpful to get practical about discipling nations; a more pointed approach to specific sectors of society is a good way to get focused and practical. I like the concept of spheres. I also think that limiting it to seven ignores how society has changed in the last 30 years. When we make something sacred out of a good principle we can create an edifice of error.

If you are married to the 7M movement, or whatever you may call it, I quote Kris Vallaton of Bethel Church in Redding, "I can think for myself; the crowd normally doesn't think that well." I am concerned that we are crowd-surfing on this topic, rather than thinking clearly. The concept of spheres of society is useful, but not foolproof. Over-excitement about seven specific spheres of society can lead to talk of a "movement" that is more driven by hype than by God. One of the purposes of this book is to see people released fully into the work that God has for them to do. I am additionally concerned that people do not get limited to one domain or sphere, and that we do not elevate the "mountains" to a status not intended in scripture. The question is not whether we are called to disciple nations; the question is how we should do this. I am genuinely concerned that, despite all the good intentions, there are dangers to the recent resurgence of "seven mountains" thinking.

I will also take you into thinking about the assets that a just God gives to all societies, and how to steward them. Separating assets and spheres can be helpful. We will then explore together the foundations of cities and societies, often spiritual in nature, and how they can be fixed if they are mislaid, burned or missing.

"By faith you can move mountains." I have always thought about this as removing the negative. Recently I understood it in a different way. By faith I can move the mountain of the Lord to whatever circumstance, situation, or sphere I am in. The needed answer is generally the same: we need more of God. Bringing the full truth of God together with the power of God to situations, quickened by the liberating work of God in Christ—by faith praying that the mountain of the Lord come to every part of life—this is what I want to be part of.

> This is God's Message to Zerubbabel: 'You can't force these things. They only come about through my Spirit,' says God-of-the-Angel-Armies. 'So, big mountain, who do you think you are? Next to Zerubbabel you're nothing but a molehill. He'll proceed to set the Cornerstone in place, accompanied by cheers: Yes! Yes! Do it!'[1]

My hope is we can glean the good and avoid the pitfalls as we work together to transform society.

Brett Johnson
Spring 2011

---

1   Zechariah 4:5-7, The Message

Synopsis

A key observation of this book is that thinking about separate spheres of society is good, but it is still a work in progress. I believe we are still in the early days of defining which spheres are essential. I am deeply concerned that, instead of empowering people, teaching on the seven mountains is trapping people, limiting them to this or that mountain, inadvertently teaching that they do not have authority in all spheres. Citizens of the kingdom of God have a passport that takes them to any mountain.

We have also done very little to distinguish spheres (or domains) from the "assets" needed in societies of varying levels of sophistication. We therefore call assets, such as technology or agriculture, a sphere just because we think it is important, and yet we are not sure where to put it. Therefore, I am calling for us to reflect on the difference between a society's assets, and its spheres. One of the reasons for this is the recognition that a just God gives all societies something to work with. Not only are they made in God's image, but also the creation around them creates unique potential to partner with God. If we are to be societal transformers, we must help societies discover and steward those assets.

> *All generalizations are false including this one; yet we keep making generalizations. We create images; graven ones that can't be changed. We dismiss or accept people, products, programs and propaganda according to the labels they come under. We know a little about something, and we treat it like we know everything.*
>
> Elizabeth Elliot
> **All That Was Ever Ours**

A third factor to note with this subject is this: we either damn it or deify it by using overly charged religious language. Instead of saying, "I thought it would be a good idea to have 9 spheres" we say, "I had a prophetically anointed revelation" which can be another way of saying, "I have a pretty good idea but I don't want to argue its merits." I am suggesting in this book such claims to revelation should not prevent inquiry, testing and proving thought.

Those who know me will attest that I am not a "middle of the road" person if middle of the road equates to "don't take a stand, try to be politically correct, and let's have everyone agree all the time." Nonetheless, a fourth thing I am calling for in this book is for us to find the road between the extremes of defeatism and dominionism, without throwing the baby out with the bath water.

A key section of the book addresses the question, "What happens on the Mountain of the Lord?"—I suggest 10 things that are part of our personal transformation to be effective agents in any sphere, and seven of these happen on The Mountain of the Lord. We cannot be a force for societal transformation without personal transformation. Logic and reason are powerful allies, but no match for the spiritual battles inherent in societal transformation.

Finally, if we become what we focus on, then we must spend time imagining what our world would look like if the glory of God permeated and was visible in all of society. I therefore try to open a few cracks through which we can peek at the glory of God in society.

With this quick snapshot behind us, let's get on to the meat of Transforming Society. I have divided the book into seven parts:

- Part 1—Spheres of Society
- Part 2—Assets of Society
- Part 3—Foundations of Societies
- Part 4—Competencies required to Transform Society
- Part 5—The Glory of God
- Part 6—Phases of Nationhood
- Part 7—Call to Action.

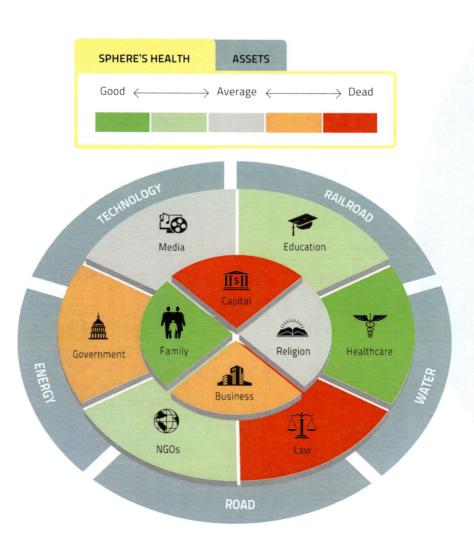

Figure 1: Every society has a number of spheres. In addition, there are assets that make up the infrastructure of a nation. Spheres must be transformed and assets must be stewarded for a society to reach its maximum potential.

In this section

History has a way of repeating itself

Good facets of mountain thinking

Detractors

The road between dominionism and defeatism

Domainationalism

Scriptures covering The Mountain of the Lord

Top-down theology

What happens on the Mountain of the Lord

The scary "-isms"

The three missing spheres

The 10 molehills explained

Where does the church fit into this?

Scrapping "Business as Missions"

Why "parachurch" is outdated

Part 1

Spheres of Society

22   Transforming Society

History has a way of repeating itself

Churches, non-profits and universities are latching onto the seven mountains story and forming their strategy around it. Books are being written to unpack the topic. Conferences abound. But does that mean everything in it is right? One of the wisest men who ever lived wrote "there is nothing new under the sun." If there is as much truth about there being "mountains" in society as the current mountain-fever would suggest, then the construct should be in the Bible, at least conceptually.

The good news is there are plenty of mountains of significance in the scriptures, one of the most common being "the mountain of the Lord." As we shall see later, this is referred to as a specific mountain in a geographical location that was frequented by God and people in the past. It is also used as a metaphor for the place we get wisdom and God's perspective; and it is spoken of as a future place that God shall establish.

In Micah 4:1-2 we read:

> [1] In the last days the mountain of the Lord's temple will be established as chief among the mountains; it will be raised above the hills, and peoples will stream to it. [2] Many nations will come and say, "Come, let us go up to the mountain of the Lord, to the house of the God of Jacob. He will teach us his ways, so that we may walk in his paths." The law will go out from Zion, the word of the Lord from Jerusalem.

The phrase, The Mountain of the Lord, is even used to refer to God himself, who is the Rock of Israel. Having said that, there is actually not much in scripture to support the popular notion of cities or societies consisting of "Seven Mountains." The only specific reference to seven hills is, in fact, a rather negative one.

Revelation 17: 8-10 says:

> [8] The beast, which you saw, once was, now is not, and will come up out of the Abyss and go to his destruction. The inhabitants of the earth whose names have not been written in the book of life from the creation of the world will be astonished when they see the beast, because he once was, now is not, and yet will come.
> [9] "This calls for a mind with wisdom. The seven heads are seven hills on which the woman sits. [10] They are also seven kings. Five have fallen, one is, the other has not yet come; but when he does come, he must remain for a little while.

These are not exactly words you want on the brochure of your 'seven mountains' conference.

This does not mean to say that there is no validity to contemplating how to advance the cause of Christ through systematic thinking about the society in which we live. Just as the concept of "ethnos" revitalized missions efforts after the Lausanne Conference in 1972, likewise the thinking on sectors of society has helped us be more deliberate about how to understand, love and transform society. It is, in some senses, a packaging of truths in a way that makes things easy to grasp. There is precedent for this in concepts such as the Four Spiritual Laws, Steps to Peace with God and other "tools" that have been helpful.

Whenever we package things up for neat consumption, however, we run the risk that in the packaging we lose the potency. There have been numerous attempts to make the notion of "discipling a nation" more comprehensible and the task of "taking a city" more practical. It may be helpful to trace some of the outlines of thought through the past centuries that have led to the present "seven mountains" stream.

In his book on worldview David K Naugle points out that "the headwaters of the worldview tradition among evangelical Protestants can be traced to two primary sources, both of which flow from the theological wellsprings of the reformer from Geneva, John Calvin (1509-1564). The first is the Scottish Presbyterian theologian, apologist, minister and educator James Orr (1844-1913). The second is the Dutch neo-Calvanist theologian and statesman, Abraham Kuyper (1837-1920)... they gave birth to an agenda to conceive of biblical faith as a robust, systemic vision of reality that opened up Christianity to full flower so that it could meet the challenges of the world head-on."

James Orr

Orr lived at a time when, according to C.S. Lewis, the West was going through "the un-christening of Europe" and this was on Orr's mind when he gave a series of lectures and in 1893 published *The Christian View of God and the World*. Orr saw life as "an ordered whole" and perceived that the onslaught against this holistic perspective was the issue.

> *The opposition which Christianity encounters... extends to the whole manner of conceiving of the world, and man's place in it, the manner of conceiving to the entire system of things, natural and moral, of which we form a part. It is no longer an opposition of detail, but of principle. It is the Christian view of things in general which is attacked, and it is by an exposition and vindication of the Christian view of things as a whole that the attack can be successfully met.*

The second part of Orr's title is critical in that he points out that the Christian Worldview is anchored in the person of Jesus Christ.

Abraham Kuijper

Another early proponent of the idea of spheres was a man who himself was multifaceted. Abraham Kuijper (generally known as Abraham Kuyper) was born in Holland and was a journalist, statesman and theologian. He founded the Anti-Revolutionary Party and was prime minister of the Netherlands between 1901 and 1905.

One facet of Kuijper's thinking that has become twisted, perhaps, is his notion of "sphere sovereignty." I believe it is fair to say he advocated that it is good to have state, church, education and business as autonomous but interconnected spheres. Separating church and state was good—but separating God and government was never the intention. Similarly, church and business had different modus operandi, but it was never his proposition to separate God and business.

Unfortunately some have interpreted "sphere sovereignty" to mean that if you belong to one sphere you have no authority in another sphere. This is clearly untrue. Jesus said, "All authority has been given to me... go in my name." A famous Kuijper quote clarifies the matter:

> *Oh, no single piece of our mental world is to be hermetically sealed off from the rest, and there is not a square inch in the whole domain of our human existence over which Christ, who is Sovereign over all, does not cry: 'Mine!'*

Dr. Francis Schaeffer

In more recent times Dr. Francis Schaeffer picked up on some of Kuijper's teaching and built on concepts of Christian world view to counter the Communist Manifesto and the Humanist Manifesto. Detractors of Schaeffer claim he was promoting a theocracy, but he cleared this up when he stated:

> *State officials must know that we are serious about stopping abortion... First, we must make definite that we are in no way talking about any kind of theocracy. Let me say that with great emphasis. Witherspoon, Jefferson, the American Founders had no idea of a theocracy. That is made plain by the First Amendment, and we must continually emphasize the fact that we are not talking about some kind, or any kind, of a theocracy.*

Although Schaeffer was not promoting a theocracy, this did not stop some Christians using his teaching as a basis for radical social action. People

Bill Bright and Loren Cunningham

took his views against secular humanism and pluralism and launched Christian social and political action groups, whether Schaeffer intended it or not.

Later Loren Cunningham and Bill Bright both sensed that God had revealed to them that there were seven spheres of society key to the discipling of a nation. The story is recorded in an interview that Os Hillman conducted with Loren Cunningham in November 2007. I quote it here:

> *It was August, 1975. My family and I were up in a little cabin in Colorado. And the Lord had given me that day a list of things I had never thought about before. He said "This is the way to reach America and nations for God. And {He said}, "You have to see them like classrooms or like places that were already there, and go into them with those who are already working in those areas." And I call them "mind-molders" or "spheres". I got the word "spheres" from II Corinthians 10 where Paul speaks in the New American Standard about the "spheres" he had been called into. And with these spheres there were seven of them, and I'll get to those in a moment. But it was a little later that day, the ranger came up, and he said, "There is a phone call for you back at the ranger's station." So I went back down, about 7 miles, and took the call. It was a mutual friend who said, "Bill Bright and Vonnette are in Colorado at the same time as you are. Would you and Darlene come over and meet with them? They would love to meet with you." So we flew over to Boulder on a private plane of a friend of ours. And as we came in and greeted each other, {we were friends for quite a while}, and I was reaching for my yellow paper that I had written on the day before. And he said, "Loren, I want to show you what God has shown me!" And it was virtually the same list that God had given me the day before. Three weeks later, my wife Darlene had seen Dr. Francis Schaeffer on TV and he had the same list! And so I realized that this was for the body of Christ.*

> *Pretty soon you will bypass your mastery of this hill or that hill and say, 'Come and let us go up to the mountain of the Lord... the chief among the mountains... raised above the hills. He will teach us his ways, so that we may walk in his paths.' You will be a top-down, mountain living, hill taming, multi-molehill son or daughter of the kingdom.*
>
> *Brett Johnson*

Others have equated the spheres of society to the gates of a city. In ancient times the way to get into a city to "take it" was through the gates or over the walls. The ancient City of Jerusalem, for example, had 17 gates.

If gates and spheres do not do it for you, perhaps you might like doors. Dr. Alistair Petrie has described 9 doors to a city and given good thought as to what makes each one different, and what we need to do to enter them. Dr. Ravi Zaccharais, a brilliant apologist, has described four spheres of society. Ed Silvoso talks about three components to the marketplace: business, education and government.

Landa Cope in her fine work on the The Old Testament Template has come up with seven or eight "spheres of influence."

This is consistent with language from the field of international relations. In California, where I live, "sphere of influence" has a legal meaning as a plan for the probable physical boundaries and service area of a local agency. Spheres of influence at California local agencies are regulated by Local Agency Formation Commissions (LAFCO). Each county in California has a LAFCO.

Marshall Foster writes of the Four Spheres of Government, namely, Individual, Family, Church and State.

My friend Bob Roberts of Northwood Church speaks of eight domains of a global society: Economics, Agriculture, Education, Medical/Science/ Technology, Communication, Arts & Entertainment, Governance & Justice, and Family. He teaches that these domains are evident on a national scale, in your state or province, and in your city. Depending on your geographic location, some domains are more prominent than others. He goes on to say, "The whole world is in flux, each domain is struggling to find itself— what an incredible opportunity for the church, or a nightmare that will lead to old metrics that no longer measure what really leads to change or old paradigms that were new 30 years ago—still based on a dream of modernity."

The highest number I have ever seen is 17 spheres of society, perhaps one for each of the ancient gates of Jerusalem. The point is not whether there are three (a biblical number), four (a biblical number), five (a biblical number), seven (another biblical number), ten (a very biblical number) or seventeen. Whichever way you slice it, and for whatever reason, it is helpful to break down the injunction to "go and make disciples of all nations" into bite-sized pieces.

Today

In more recent times Os Hillman and Johnny Enlow have revived the domain discussion under the label of The Seven Mountains. 'Apostolic' groups have picked up on this and there is much activity in teaching, conferences and even talk of movements. Lance Wallnau has a 7M University.

How is it then, that "The Seven Mountains" has grown in popularity recently? Maybe it is God, and maybe it is good marketing. Perhaps it is truth standing on its own two feet; and perhaps it is plenty of people jumping on the next Christian bandwagon. This may sound irreverent, but we need to be aware that we live in a time when we have the media to promote concepts to a worldwide audience, and this adds a responsibility to be careful about what we propagate. A client of mine described e-mail to me as "spreading darkness at the speed of light." With the Internet we are able to take concepts and spread them like wildfire. Webcasting, podcasting, twittering and Facebooking allow us to grab ideas and quickly have them take on a life of their own.

We must therefore be prepared to peel back the covers and examine things from many perspectives so that we can indeed "rightly divide the word of truth." I am not saying in this book that teaching on the mountains is bad. I am saying that we must beware of the shortcomings that can creep into such teaching and make sure that we don't miss the forest for the trees—or the mountain for the molehills.

Scripture does indeed refer to mountains... my question is, "Whose mountain do you want to focus on?" The spheres of society are relative molehills when compared to the mountain of the Lord!

In his book, **Face to Face with God**, Bill Johnson says, "It is not healthy to have a big devil and a small (impractical) God. It is not that the devil has no power or should be ignored... we just can't afford to be impressed by the one who is restricted in power when we serve an all-powerful God. I try to live in such a way that nothing ever gets bigger than my awareness of God's presence." We need to live in such a way that no mountain ever gets bigger than the mountain of the Lord. After all, we need a face-to-face encounter with God if we are to truly tackle the four, seven or seventeen molehills.

You may remember the film titled *The Englishman Who Went Up a Hill But Came Down a Mountain*. In the movie, two English cartographers visit the small South Wales village of Ffynnon Garw, to measure what is claimed to be the "first mountain inside of Wales." It was set in 1917 when the war in Europe was in full swing. The villagers were very proud of their "mountain" and were understandably disappointed and furious to find that it is in fact a "hill." Not to be outwitted by a rule (and the Englishmen who enforce it), the villagers set out to make their hill into a mountain... and the story continues from there. I am a little concerned that we have taken hills and, with much scurrying back and forth with buckets of advertising and wheelbarrows of hyperbole, have made hills into mountains. Our intent is good, but we have become preoccupied with our hills instead of glorying in the God of the mountain from which we get our identity.

Good facets of mountain thinking

I already mentioned that I believe that Wisdom supersedes domains or sub-domains. Nonetheless there are many good aspects to thinking about mountains, spheres or domains. For one, it helps us to get **focused**. God is infinite, and we are finite. If we try to do everything in general we run the risk of doing nothing in particular.

A second benefit is **deepened love** for the sphere. In order to disciple something you have to love it. We cannot sit on one mountain and lob mortars to another mountain and hope to transform it. We have to be on it, understand it, and love it before we can transform it. I am particularly aware of traditional missionaries and church people who want to disciple business or media, for example, but they do not love business or media. Many years ago I told a friend in a traditional missions organization that spoke a lot about discipling nations and business, "You cannot disciple what you do not love."

A third benefit is developing a **deeper understanding**. While someone has said "specialization is a consequence of the fall of man" we, as individuals, cannot be all things to all people all the time. When we slice the facets of society into manageable elements then we can do deeper research; but we must remember that it all ties together at the end of the day. Understanding specific domains helps us go from generalists with good intentions, to people with a deeper love and understanding of a specific arena.

A fourth benefit—and these are not in order of importance—is that people in each sphere, are validated as ministers. I love it when politicians understand that they are ministers of a greater government. When healthcare pioneers realize that they are apostles, when media people figure out that they are prophets... then the 95% of the church that is traditionally on the bench become active players. Isaiah 61:6 puts it this way: "And you will be called priests of the Lord, you will be named ministers of our God."

A fifth benefit is the **gathering of like-minded people**. We struggled in Cape Town when we were working with three smaller businesses in the Media sector. The challenge was helping them find their God-given business purpose. Once we put them together and asked "what would it look like if Jesus were running Media in Cape Town?" They found their joint purpose. A follow on reason why I like the sphere concept is that it can result in the **cross-cultural mobilization** of people. I spoke with a South African member of parliament about repurposing government. He said, "There are Christians in every political party in South Africa but we will never get them to agree." I told him that there is a way to do it. "If we gather believers from every political party and deploy them to another nation to share principles of godly government, then they will have to submit to the word of God as they prepare to go."

A seventh reason for thinking about mountains (or molehills) is **joint strategy development**. Unity is a big factor in praying together, finding God's strategy, and sharing resources. "Two can put ten thousand to flight."

A good example, perhaps, of focused thinking about different spheres is the Quick Reference Chart at the back of Johnny Enlow's book. It enables readers to think about distinct facets of mountains which he has tied to the enemies that Israel faced in the Promised Land.

An illustrative extract follows[2]:

MOUNTAIN	ENEMY	PRINCIPALITY	SIGNIFICANT DISPLAYING AUTHORITY	BASIC MISSION	REV 5:12 KEY
Media	Hittities	Apolloyon	Evangelists	Fill airwaves with good news	Blessing
Education	Amorites (humanism)	Beelzebub (lies)	Teachers	Bring new curriculum	Wisdom

If you read Deuteronomy 7 you will find that God's remedy for the seven nations—the Hittites, Girgashites, Amorites, Canaanites, Perizzites, Hivites and Jebusites—was destruction. Logically, if the spheres of society are equivalent to the seven mountains which draw from these seven nations we should be out to destroy the spheres of society. We should be turning seven mountains into a flat plane. Deuteronomy 7:5 makes it

2   Ibid, page 190, 191–The Seven Mountain Prophecy

clear: "This is what you are to do to them: Break down their altars, smash their sacred stones, cut down their Asherah poles and burn their idols in the fire."

If, however, we understand that these nations are representative of the spiritual forces that oppose the advancement of the kingdom of God... if we remember that the precedent for God's instruction regarding the seven nations was the destruction of the gods of Egypt... if we see that the principle here is that "we wrestle not against flesh and blood" then we will not draw the wrong conclusion from the text. It is not about seven; it is about any spiritual force that sets up a system that operates in opposition to God. The seven mountain prophecy language is fine for understanding the principle that there are little gods that need, like the idols of old, to be torn down in spiritual warfare. But it is not exhaustive—remember the plagues in Egypt and the gods that were destroyed just to get Israel out of that foreign system—we have to blend in the workings of the kingdom as demonstrated and taught by Jesus to get a full picture.

In summary, there are many advantages of understanding spheres of society: focus, understanding, recognizing spiritual underpinnings, etc. But there are also dangers.

Detractors

Unfortunately we live in a world where what you have for breakfast will be analyzed for nutritional value on someone's blog by tea time. The good part about this is that when we stray towards error there will be an army of people ready to take us out with "friendly fire." If you study the area of spheres, sphere sovereignty and societal transformation you will quickly realize that there are dangers to this truth. Taken to the wrong extreme the teaching on "your kingdom come" can be taken to mean that Jesus will establish his rule and reign on earth now by overtaking the systems and governments of this world... soon. When one states it in black and white, it seems unlikely. It also reminds us of the Jewish religious leaders who missed the here and now of Jesus because he did not overthrow the Roman government.

Detractors will label the theology of those who seek to extend the kingdom of God by working in specific sectors as "dominionism" and "theonomy" and "Christian reconstructionism."

I want to be clear that I do not believe everything that the anti-dominionism camp says. In order to make their arguments they tend to extract pieces of what people say, string them together, and make it sound like some are saying that Jesus is coming back to head up the Klu Klux

Klan. They accuse those who speak of mountains and domains as leading a peaceful revolution to change things on earth now by getting Christians and the truths they espouse into leadership in all sectors of society.

They say that "dominionists" hope for a domino theory that if we get enough people into the right positions fighting for truth, then the kingdom of God will happen here and now. The counter argument from the mountain people is that the "just get people saved" group are arguing that if we get enough people coming to salvation, then when a critical mass of people have been saved, then the world will be a better place by sheer force of numbers. The mountain people argue that this has simply not been the case in history. It was 'saved' people in Rwanda (with a population of Christians of over 80%) who conducted ethnic cleansing, for example. More saved people do not necessarily "make disciples of all nations."

One of the core issues is the interpretation of the word "dominion" in Genesis 1. We hear "rule, reign, be the boss, conquer, subdue" but we are less prone to hear "serve, steward, manage as caretakers."

> *There are large challenges in every society. The physical giants encountered by Israel — Goliath and his friends — were also symbolic of the spiritual giants they faced, and that we still face today. Every nation, every sphere and every city has giants. It is not the job of Government to fight all giants, because the first responsibility is with God's people.*
>
> Brett Johnson

What we also somehow miss is the clear truth that prior to the fall of man into sin, man did not rule over man. Genesis 1:26 says, "Then God said, 'Let us make man in our image, in our likeness, and let them rule over the fish of the sea and the birds of the air, over the livestock, over all the earth, and over all the creatures that move along the ground.'" What is missing from this verse? It does not say that man was to rule over man, and if we turn the taking of mountains into a crusade-like cry, we will miss our mandate to serve.

When we propose that there are spheres of society that need to be influenced, we must be careful to not interpret this as "ruled" or "dominioned" rather than served.

Genesis 2:4-5 says:

> When the Lord God made the earth and the heavens—and no shrub of the field had yet appeared on the earth and no plant of the field had yet sprung up, for the Lord God had not sent rain on the earth *and there was no man to work [till, serve] the ground...*

Gregory Boyd has written a book titled **The Myth of a Christian Nation** and he claims that the job of Christians is to follow the example of Jesus, not take over political parties. Boyd writes in his introduction, "Because the myth that America is a Christian nation has led many to associate America with Christ, many now hear the Good News of Jesus only as American news, capitalistic news, imperialistic news, exploitative news, anti-gay news, or Republican news. And whether justified or not, many people want nothing to do with it."

In an interview with Charlie Rose he says, "I am not surprised that politicians use political rhetoric... What grieves me is that such large segments of the church don't realize what's going on and get co-opted into a political agenda. Jesus never once allowed the politics of the day to set his agenda. He always turned their 'kingdom of the world' questions into his questions."

Christianity Today summarized the situation in an article by James K.A. Smith in October 2006.

> *In the early 1970s, some influential voices began to argue that this understanding of the church's calling was truncated. In particular, Ron Sider and Jim Wallis argued for a more holistic approach to the gospel, noting that Jesus' model for ministry attended to concrete, "worldly" matters of poverty and illness as occasions for redemption (Luke 4:14-20).*

> *At the same time, Richard Mouw, from a Reformed perspective, invited evangelicals to see the dualism of the status quo: that their concern with souls and eternity ignored God's affirmation of the goodness of bodies and the temporal world. By ignoring politics and culture, evangelicals were unwittingly giving over these spheres of creation to forces of distortion and destruction, rather than redemptively redirecting them. Mouw invited evangelicals to take up the cultural mandate as a complement to, and expression of, the Great Commission.*

> *But a funny thing happened on the way to the Capitol. If Wallis, Sider, and Mouw were trying to pull evangelicals away from their*

isolationism, they likely didn't anticipate the way in which the pendulum would swing the other way. In fact, evangelicals today have became such zealous converts to the cultural mandate that one can argue it has nearly trumped the Great Commission. Christian leaders spend more time worrying about activist judges, Venezuelan dictators, and constitutional amendments than their forbears could ever have imagined. Devoting themselves to political strategizing and superintending the machinations of government, evangelicals have so embraced participation in the "earthly city" that one wonders whether they've lost their passport to the City of God. Or worse: Some suspect that evangelicals in America have collapsed the two, confusing the City of God with America as a city set on a hill.

While Boyd believes that everything about him is infused with his faith in Christ. He is pro-life to the core, he is opposed to violence... a conservative Christian. But he does not believe that this translates into a particular vote. "My book is a call for the Church to look like Jesus serving the world." Charlie Rose challenged him about whether this should translate into action. Boyd agreed that it should... but the rub comes when you try to get specific about what that looks like. He highlights the difficulty of carving a middle road.

The road between dominionism and defeatism

The flip side of *dominion theology*, as detractors call things, is *defeatist theology*. This is the idea that "things are going to hell in a hand basket, but I have a one way ticket to heaven so I don't need to worry." This line of reasoning goes on to say, "Not only do I not need to worry, but there is no sense in making things better now because pretty soon Jesus is coming back, and he will fix it all when he returns." No need to recycle, not much cause to worry about alternative energy, and little sense in trying to change laws and elect godly leaders. "We are in the world but not of the world" is the general theme. "The best we can do is to get people to make a spiritual decision to accept Christ as Savior, be nice, and go to heaven one day."

If this sounds like a polarized position, it is! In fact, the proponents and detractors of any position make the other side sound a little loony. Things are presented as an either-or proposition. The reality is, at least in my thinking, that God is the God of AND. "Jerusalem AND Judea AND Samaria AND the ends of the earth." He is the God of "Abraham AND Isaac AND Jacob." He makes his sun shine on the righteous AND the unrighteous.

Somewhere between "we cannot change much now" and "we will make everything perfect before Jesus returns" is a road many of us travel. It is not dominionism, and it is not defeatism. It is not "one day pie in the sky when we die" and it is not "all things under his feet right now." It is a path of responsibly putting our faith into action so that today Jesus gets the fruit of his work on our behalf. It is a road where we seek to see the implications of "God… was in Christ reconciling the world [cosmos] to himself" worked out in all of life. It is all his, he deserves to see it come back into alignment with the will of the Father, and every believer has a responsibility to ask, "Father, what would it look like for everything in my world to align with You and Your ways?"

In the previously quoted *Christianity Today* article Smith goes on to disagree with Boyd and points out the problem of an either-or approach. "While the difference between these [two kingdoms] is important—it's exactly what is forgotten in the God-and-country, Constantinian approach—Boyd's framing of an absolute dichotomy lacks insight. In particular, Boyd can't seem to imagine a good earthly kingdom, which indicates an inadequate theology of creation and an under-developed imagination. Boyd's relegation of politics to a matter of indifference means that, ultimately, Christ's call to discipleship doesn't touch the public square. His constant refrain is simply to "vote your conscience"—which points to the persistent individualism that dominates his account."

Smith concludes with this thought: "So is Boyd simply inviting us back to pietism? I'm afraid so. My question is: Can evangelical thinking about cultural engagement leave behind the either/or of Constantinian triumphalism vs. Pietistic retreat? To escape an oscillation between these two unbiblical extremes, we must nurture a more nuanced and creative political imagination."

The answer is not found, however, in re-locating dichotomy to the fertile ground of domains.

Domainationalism

There is a real danger that our prior problems of denominationalism get replaced with what I call "domainationalism." Rather than boxing people according to their theological beliefs, we now box them according to their domains. God is not a God in a box, and he does not expect his people to be boxed in. The sooner that we realize that sinful man tends towards control the better. We often place labels on people to contain them rather than to release them. I am all for understanding where people should focus on a particular sector such as business or government or whatever sphere it may be. But by doing this I have no desire to limit them from functioning in other spheres.

In our desire to be helpful we ask people to focus on one sphere or another. Focus is generally a good thing. It becomes a bad thing, however, when it becomes a disempowerer, rather than an empowerer. It is fair to evaluate where you most experience God's favor. If you see more of his blessing in your life when you are serving in a particular field, then work where God is giving you favor. But make sure you don't develop a theology that says you are limited to this or that mountain.

I was at a conference a few years ago and met a proponent of the seven mountains of society. As soon as he met me he asked, "Which mountain are you from?" The implication was clear: people are from one mountain or the other. More recently I was speaking about my book **Convergence** to a group of students. At the end there was a question time and the first inquiry had nothing to do with the topic of the day, but was "How do I know what mountain I am from?" I explained quite simply that, as a kingdom person, she was from the mountain of the Lord. She was relieved because she had been feeling a pressure to have her mountain chosen, settled on, and in the theological bag.

If you are a kingdom person your authority comes from The Mountain of the Lord, and not from a molehill. You have authority over domains, and you do not need a passport to traverse from one to the other. Your main criteria for ministering here or there is that God sent you. That's it. If you are teaching on the spheres of society, please be careful that you do not place people in a new box. I know your heart is to release people, but we can inadvertently pigeon hole them instead.

Scriptures covering The Mountain of the Lord

There are three major passages that mention the mountain of the Lord. Before we get to these let's take note of a variety of other verses that make mention of the topic. Note from these verses that the mountain of the Lord seems to be wherever God shows up, rather than one specific geographic location. Later there are specific references to Jerusalem.

> So Abraham called that place The Lord Will Provide. And to this day it is said, "On the mountain of the Lord it will be provided."[3]

> The Lord said to Aaron, "Go into the desert to meet Moses." So he met Moses at the mountain of God and kissed him.[4]

> You will bring them in and plant them on the mountain of your inheritance—the place, O Lord, you made for your dwelling, the sanctuary, O Lord, your hands established.[5]

3   Genesis 22:14
4   Exodus 4:27
5   Exodus 15:17

So they set out from the mountain of the Lord and travelled for three days. The ark of the covenant of the Lord went before them during those three days to find them a place to rest.[6]

Great is the Lord, and most worthy of praise, in the city of our God, his holy mountain.[7]

In the last days the mountain of the Lord's temple will be established as chief among the mountains; it will be raised above the hills, and all nations will stream to it.
Many peoples will come and say, "Come, let us go up to the mountain of the Lord, to the house of the God of Jacob. He will teach us his ways, so that we may walk in his paths." The law will go out from Zion, the word of the Lord from Jerusalem.[8]

They will neither harm nor destroy on all my holy mountain, for the earth will be full of the knowledge of the Lord as the waters cover the sea.[9]

And you will sing as on the night you celebrate a holy festival; your hearts will rejoice as when people go up with flutes to the mountain of the Lord, to the Rock of Israel.[10]

And they will bring all your brothers, from all the nations, to my holy mountain in Jerusalem as an offering to the Lord—on horses, in chariots and wagons, and on mules and camels," says the Lord. "They will bring them, as the Israelites bring their grain offerings, to the temple of the Lord in ceremonially clean vessels."[11]

In the last days the mountain of the Lord's temple will be established as chief among the mountains; it will be raised above the hills, and peoples will stream to it. Many nations will come and say, "Come, let us go up to the mountain of the Lord, to the house of the God of Jacob. He will teach us his ways, so that we may walk in his

6   Numbers 10:33
7   Psalm 48:1
8   Isaiah 2:2-3
9   Isaiah 11:9
10   Isaiah 30:29
11   Isaiah 66:20

> paths." The law will go out from Zion, the word of the Lord from Jerusalem.[12]

These passages refer to various things: first, there is a specific place (a mountain in Jerusalem); then to a time when the knowledge of God will be everywhere (Isaiah 11:9); there is also the metaphor of the Person of God himself (the Rock of Israel). One might say that the mountain of the Lord is the kingdom of God... but I think there is more to it than that. The kingdom encompasses everything. The mountain of the Lord is the place where we meet with God—not a physical place necessarily—and get transformed in his presence. Transformed people transform people. So the mountain of the Lord can be any place where we encounter God. It can be alone, or in a group. It can be one special place, and it can be us learning to welcome God's presence into every place where we go.

12   Micah 4:1-2

Top-down theology

A place of perspective

In today's terms we speak of having a perspective and praxis that understands heaven and attempts to walk out on earth what we see the Father doing in heaven. John 5:19 is key: "I only do what I see the Father doing." Our trouble is that we have difficulty seeing what the Father is doing; and we will have difficulty seeing what he is doing unless we sit on his mountain. It behoves us to learn his ways. When we become mountain people then the spheres of society are not trivialized, but they become relative molehills.

Another way to grasp the nettle of the mountain matter is to consider two alternate perspectives. The first is the bottom-up perspective and it goes something like this:

> "I work my way up this mountain, then I work my way up that mountain... then I finally discover my real mountain, conquer it, and come to convergence."

This is based on the rationale that each of us has been called to one mountain or another. The truth is that we have been called to follow Jesus, not pick mountains. The apostle Paul, for example, worked across many mountains including Religion, Government, Law, Education and Business. When he got less than a warm welcome in the Religion sector, he shifted to the marketplace. When he worked in the marketplace he caused a stir, was arrested, appealed to Caesar, and was automatically in the Legal sector. His writings were highly educational, although it is less clear that he focused on this area in his later life.

In God's interactions with the Israelites and Moses it is clear that God wanted the whole nation to have a mountain experience. They opted out and effectively said to Moses, "You go to the mountain for us." They got the rules from the mountain, and Moses got to know the God of the mountain. The mountain of the Lord is the place where we meet with God, commune with him, and receive the empowerment needed for our ongoing assignment. We get instruction as well, but without the empowerment the instruction is futile.

> When the people saw the thunder and lightning and heard the trumpet and saw the mountain in smoke, they trembled with fear. They stayed at a distance and said to Moses, "Speak to us yourself and we will listen. But do not have God speak to us or we will die." Moses said to the people, "Do not be afraid. God has come to test you,

> so that the fear of God will be with you to keep you from sinning." The people remained at a distance, while Moses approached the thick darkness where God was.[13]

We should not be people who say, "When I have conquered this or that mountain, then I will be closer to God." Rather we should be a people that live "top-down." In other words we should seek the face of God, learning his ways, and then doing whatever he says.

As Micah put it, "In the last days the mountain of the Lord's temple will be established as chief among the mountains; it will be raised above the hills, and peoples will stream to it." We have to be careful that the hype about the seven mountains does not overshadow that which is "chief"— preeminent, prominent, highest, foremost—among the mountains. Let's be sure we do not apply bottom-up logic to establish a top-down kingdom.

What happens on the Mountain of the Lord

There is a paradox that we need to embrace. We get supernatural equipping to tackle the molehills on the mountain of the Lord, yet we often have to put in our time on the molehills themselves in order to be effective there. When Jeremiah heard of the plight of Israel he "sat where they sat" and mourned for seven days. As indicated earlier, we can only disciple what we love. I believe we are most effective when we work in a sphere and disciple it from the inside out. This is not an absolute truth, however, as God can have us work across molehills.

So what are some of the activities that happen on the mountain of the Lord?

> He will teach us his ways, so that
> we may walk in his paths.

Learning the ways of God is a lifelong endeavor. It can, however, be dramatically accelerated when we get mountain vision. This is vague language, I know, but when we start to spend time with God with the express intent that he teach us his ways, then we get a level of equipping that approaches the Wisdom found in scripture and personified in Jesus. If we don't seek this wisdom, if we busy ourselves but don't seek God himself, we will resort to human wisdom even if Jesus is our ticket to heaven.

13 Exodus 20:18-21

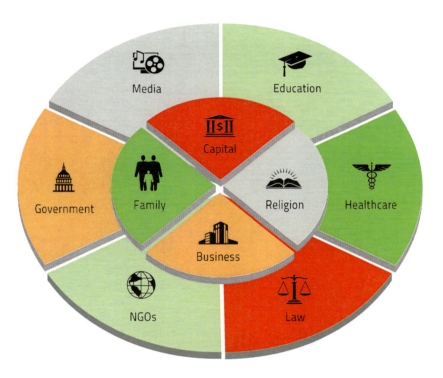

Figure 2: This figure shows all ten spheres of society with differing degrees of importance (the inner circle being more critical in this nation) and the health of each sphere (the color coding), from Dead to Good

I am not decrying study and careful thought. In fact, there are two things, at least, that can be done in preparing to tackle the 10 molehills that happen with basic hard work—you can get these *without* going to the mountain of the Lord.

1. **Education**: one can be educated in God's word and about the spheres with which you feel some affinity.

2. **Equipping & Experience**: one can gain experience in a particular sector by working in it; doing some time in a sphere is often part of the Skills Building season.[14]

There are other things that we need to do that require more than a decision of the will and an education of the mind. No amount of study or human effort will make up for these remaining things. What do we get on the mountain of the Lord that we do not just get in a classroom?

3. **Entering** God's presence. When we start encountering God we get transformed and gain a capacity to receive revelation that informs our view of the world. Without this the matter of societal transformation will, at best, be fueled by Christian Humanism rather than radical kingdom living. We need, as Ephesians says, a "spirit of wisdom and revelation." We get revelation, in part, by appropriating the access that Jesus has made for us into the presence of the Father.

4. **Encountering** God's heart for the sphere. God has done it all: he is in Government, Media, Health Care, Law, Family... you name it. Whatever spheres you can come up with, God is already there. So how does he feel about each sphere? You will never know until you go to the mountain of the Lord. We must develop God's heart for a sphere before we attempt to modify it to suit our way of thinking. The old adage is true: they don't care how much we know until they know how much we care.

5. **Experiencing** God's power. We can tackle our mountains/molehills as Moses did when he was 40 years old, or we can do so as he did after a desert encounter with the Living God. The things God has called me to tackle require a close encounter with God of a supernatural kind in order to even move towards them. Let's face it, none of us can say to a mountain, "Be cast into the sea" in our own authority. None of us can bring about sustainable change simply with human effort. The words we speak must be backed up by a

14   I cover this topic in the book, Convergence. Indaba Publishing

demonstration of the power of God. Each sphere may need different miracles, but they will indeed need miracles.

6. **Enlightenment**: There is information, then there is revelation. God expects you to "study to show yourself approved" and this takes, well, study. But there is a huge difference between fact-finding, head-pounding research and spiritual revelation. Some things are only seen in the context of the Spirit. Don't you love it when God pulls you away, even for five minutes at your desk in your office, for a mountain experience where he enlightens you?

7. **Encouragement**: tackling even molehills is not for wienies. It takes courage to face the giants in each sector of society. Part of God's strategy is to put us in situations that are difficult and clearly beyond our ability to cope in the natural. We need encouragement. I am grateful for my friends who encourage me, challenge me and spur me on. I have times, as we all do, when I have to go to God for myself, by myself. I need to have the Father's words, "Be of good courage" echoing in my ears as I head towards the giants. If Jesus needed to go to his mountain to draw courage, surely we need to do the same.

8. **Endorsement**. Get endorsed by God. We cannot be trusted with a molehill when we are still seeking the endorsement of man. When we go up the mountain we should be attentive to hearing God's endorsement. "This is my beloved son." When Moses asked, "How will they know you have sent me?" It was a pretty good question. We need to come down the mountain knowing that God has spoken his endorsement of us. When Jesus was on the Mount of Transfiguration the endorsing voice from heaven said, "This is my beloved son; listen to him." Mountain people are endorsed people.

9. **Enthusiasm**, excitement. Sometimes we discourage weekend retreats and other mountain top experiences. When the early disciples came from a God encounter people could see that they had been with Jesus. Tackling molehills requires that the God we have known on the mountain overflow through us onto those in the valley. *Enthusia* means "a god within" – we have the God of the Universe within us. We need to be genuinely excited about God. Ah, you may be saying, "This is too emotional, and we have to walk by faith not emotions." If you are truly going to go up against the giants that inhabit the molehills you better have a mountain experience to remember or your heart will indeed melt like wax. You will be better off with an unmistakable encounter with God so that, when faced with the opposition, you will say to yourself, "I remember my encounter with God; it was as real as the nails on my fingers; and he has sent me into this arena." You will need the enthusiasm from the

mountain because under the molehill is a hole that can drain your courage quicker than you think.

10. **Enjoy** the view from the mountain. Dr. Martin Luther King said, "I have been to the mountain, and I have seen the Promised Land." Tomorrow may look hard, so spend time looking into the future. The best view is from the mountain of the Lord. Those involved in changing the world regularly need encouragement; enjoy the view when you see glimpses of what could be.

I have not really described the activities of the mountain of the Lord that much, more the outcomes of being there. I sense there may be some danger in being too prescriptive about what happens on the mountain of the Lord. We are prone to formulate, we want systems that work. The mountain of the Lord is about him, his presence, whatever he wants, and not about us and our methods and our ways. Some have gone to the book of Revelation and said words to this effect: "The mountain of the Lord is heaven, and what happens in heaven is 24x7 worship, so prayer rooms are the mountain of the Lord." It is true that there will be continuous worship in heaven. What else will there be? Work? Ruling and reigning? Dancing? No sleep? No marriage? Will those people wanting to emulate heaven on earth stop eating, sleeping, and marrying while they have a 24x7 worship time?

Yet it is true that praise is key to God's dominion. Psalm 22 expresses this well.

> 1 My God, my God, why have you forsaken me? Why are you so far from saving me, so far from the words of my groaning? 2 O my God, I cry out by day, but you do not answer, by night, and am not silent. 3 Yet you are enthroned as the Holy One; you are the praise of Israel. [or] Yet you are holy, enthroned on the praises of Israel.

The psalm goes on to explain true dominion in verse 28: "dominion belongs to the Lord and he rules over the nations."

This is a psalm that prophesies Christ's death on the cross, and provides the keys of how he survived that ordeal. Praise, praise, praise. I am not questioning the connection between praise and God's presence, but I am saying that prayer rooms are not *the only* expression of the mountain of the Lord, although they can be one of them.

The scary "-isms"

Whenever we subdivide the kingdom of God into territories we feed the monster of dichotomy. There are two territories: the kingdom of light and the kingdom of darkness. There are two sides: for God, and against God. The dividing lines between kings, priests, men, women, Jews, Greeks etc. were obliterated by the work of Christ on the cross.

No matter how many hills we see on our horizon, we have to clearly see the danger that each hill wants to become the highest peak. We could add a refrain to **Animal Farm**: "All domains are equal, but some domains are more equal than others." Gottfried Hetzer describes the world system as follows:

> *It is a system, built and maintained by unbelievers, and hosted, encouraged and promoted by satan. This system is supposed to manage and cater perfectly for all aspects of our lives without help or interference from God.*[15]

In every sphere we try to set up something that does not need God, and inevitably replace the one true God with little gods at best, or their demonic support at worst. Recognizing this tendency of man to make our doctrine, our department or our domain the center of the universe is really important. Let's take a moment to consider what happens when anything other than God gets to the center of society. There are 10 scary "-isms" that become apparent when any sphere puts itself in the place reserved only for Jesus.

SPHERE	SCARY "-ISM"
1. Government	**Statism**. We saw what happens when the state becomes God in communist countries. The same things happen in any nation where the state oversteps its bounds and takes up God's space. The interventionism in many countries can lead to statism. As believers we pray for leaders and honor those who serve in government, but we cannot adopt a philosophy that looks to Government and not God as the solution.
2. Education	**Idealism**. Here human logic is exalted and an idol can be made of the mind. Humanism is the little god of education. Developing our minds to their full potential in Christ is wonderful. Elevating rationalism above relationship with God is not only wrong, but sinful. Of course it does not look that blatant, but where we think that mankind can be educated beyond our sinful nature we get into idealism.

15   Finances – Who is in control? Gottfried Hetzer

SPHERE	SCARY "-ISM"
3. Healthcare	Determinism. When healthcare decides to play god it decides who is born, and when people should die. The value of life is determined based on warped criteria, and we quickly forget that we are made in the image of God and have value and worth simply by virtue of the fact that God was willing to send Christ to die for us. Of course we want to see progress in medical science, but we don't want healthcare at the center of society.
4. Law	Legalism. There is a difference between justice and law. The increase of lawsuits and laws can be because we look to the letter of the law and ignore the God who is the ultimate Judge and Advocate. When we make a god of our legal systems rather than making the legal system serve the constitution and constituents of a nation, and the God who inspired the foundational principles of the nation, then we run the risk of looking to our laws and not our Lawgiver.
5. Arts, Media, Entertainment	Relativism. When media is king it wants to rewrite the conscience of man with 'anything goes'—anything except God. God wants to run a highlighter over his characteristics that he has placed in man, and in all of his creation. He wants to draw out the best, polishing our many facets so that we more clearly reflect his nature. Media, when clawing for a spot at the center, becomes the new definer of truth, values and cultural norms. Absolutes give way to relatives, and the firm anchor of truth begins to drift.
6. Business	Pragmatism. When business is king we create products with no social value, and we exalt profits above virtue. Pragmatism tells the church to stay out of business, as happened recently in the UK when criticism was leveled at the banking profession by those in the Church. When we confuse the true nature of capitalism with an unbridled, value-less exaltation of wealth creation at any cost we justify actions that are unjustifiable. We make stupid statements such as, "that's just the way business works." The pure gives way to the pragmatic, the end justifies the means, and business becomes the center of society. We may call it an upturn, a boom, or God's favor... but we must make sure that we have not traded the God of the Bible for Mammon.
7. Capital	Capitalism. Not capitalism in its truest form where it creates wealth and grows the pie, but capitalism that extols the amassing of wealth by the few at the expense of the many, which is really greed, not true capitalism (So I speak here of greed masquerading as capitalism. Mammon is the main force behind this... avarice deified.) Building wealth is not wrong: deifying greed certainly is. How may Christians do you know who were in a mess because the stock markets crashed, revealing where they had placed their trust?

SPHERE	SCARY "-ISM"
8. Family	**Tribalism.** Africa is plagued by tribalism at the group level while America is plagued by anarchy at the individual level. These are the extremes where my group/family is supreme, or where I am supreme. **Nepotism** and narcissism are both ugly gods. Family is important to God, make no mistake. He is the father from whom all mankind takes its name. Households are meant to be a beautiful representation of the organic family of God. But when we elevate family above Him, shifting it to the center—and we sometimes do this as Christians—then we can slip into tribalism, individualism, or narcissism.
9. NGOs (Non-Governmental Organizations)	**Causism.** This could be environmentalism, feminism, socialism (often more an elitist cause than a truly held philosophy)... whatever-causism. NGOs play a critical role in society. This is not new. In the early Church it is estimated that the Church in Constantinople cared for 50,000 widows and orphans. But when we think that NGOs can solve the world's problems without God, we have another form of taking matters into our own hands where we think we can do a better job than God. It is not about the environment, or slavery, or human trafficking or hunger or malaria, but about what is at the center of society.
10. Religion	**Controlism.** Even good faith can turn into bad religion. Jesus saved his best criticism for the religious leaders who should have known better than to bottle life in a system and sell it to the unsuspecting. Denominations carve out territory in this world where religion is at the center. History has many instances where churches wanted to play God, and the results were devastating. There are nations today where religious leaders run the country. Surely this is not what we are aiming at in seeking societal transformation. Another way to describe this is control. It often looks loving, subtle or benign, but when we put man in control instead of God, then we cause far reaching destruction in the lives of people and societies.

We have already seen that God, through his presence, can make any place a "mountain." We also know that work is ministry, that we do our work as worship, that everything—all of life—is God's, and that we carry his presence into every circumstance. So, in my view, to equate the mountain of the Lord to any one expression of the kingdom of God, be it houses of prayer or something else, is cutting a narrow slice off the concept, but missing the bigger whole. Why is it that we get stuck on places and systems while the era in which we live is one where each of us is the temple of the Holy Spirit? Since we have come into a relationship with God through Jesus Christ and now have his presence within us, let's make any mountain his mountain.

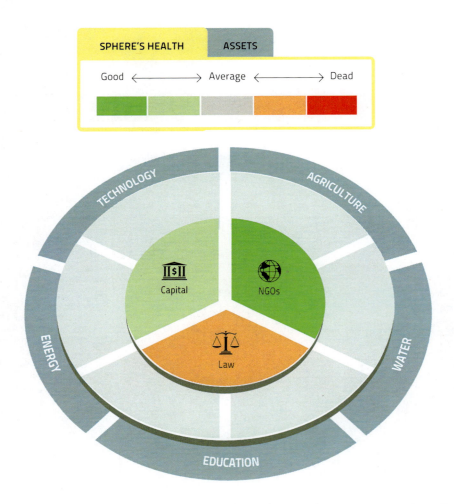

Figure 3: The Spheres of a Society: this figure highlights the three spheres usually missing in traditional definitions of society, namely, Capital, an independent judiciary (Law), and NGOs. The outer circle shows illustrative Assets of Society.

The three missing spheres

The confusing thing about working in the world of faith is many people see the perspective they have gained as having come from specific revelation from God. We are, myself in particular, peculiar people. Some even claim that they themselves are the personal successors to the people who got the original revelation about the "seven mountains." We end up giving the

Spheres of Society 49

seven mountains, seven habits, or seven seasons a ranking close to The 10 Commandments.

There are obvious challenges with this, one being that it does not allow for what one could call progressive revelation. Perhaps seven spheres was a good analysis back in the 1970s, but the world has changed since then, and even the specific definitions of the seven spheres has "floated" over time. For example, I have seen "church" as a sphere, and it has morphed to "religion." I have seen things come and go from lists, like "communication," generally added by those in the communication business.

My basis for segmenting the spheres of society has nothing to do with where people have authority, or the 17 gates of Jerusalem, or the notorious seven mountains of the book of Revelation. It fully acknowledges that there are groups and sub-groups, just as in industry segments. When Jesus explained the concept of wineskins, I believe he was alluding to the operating model of an organization or entity. The old operating model of organized religion could not contain the new, dynamic product of the kingdom of God. The wineskin is not sacred: it is what gets the wine from the producer to the consumer.

I recently visited the Guinness brewery in Ireland. Arthur Guinness was an ardent believer who refined a product—a beer originally called porter— that would be nutritious and make people full before they got drunk. Ingenious. At one point Guinness had hundreds of men working in their cooperage, making barrels. Today there are none. Why? Because 250 years later Guinness remains in the beer business, not the barrel business. The barrel is simply a wineskin, and the barrel is no longer the best way to ship product. I believe that we can argue that when an aspect of society has a significantly different wineskin (or operating model) then we could treat it as a separate sphere of society that warrants specific attention.

Guinness still impacts the nation of Ireland, but its roots are all but forgotten. I asked Guinness employees, "Do you know why Arthur Guinness developed the beer?" They were clueless. The Guinness corporation has lost sight of the founder's purpose which included a deliberate extending of the kingdom of God through a business. This week I met with friends going to China with a mission organization... founded by Guinness.

The second reason for considering three additional mountains (at least) is the fact that, in missiological terms, the characteristics of the "people groups" or ethnos are vastly different for these three additional groups. It is a generally accepted best practice to reach a people group from within that people group. A people group is defined as "the largest number of people through which the gospel can travel without having to cross a major barrier." My view is that work has become ubiquitous and the boundaries between work, and home, and church and leisure have been blurring for many years. Globalization goes well beyond trade and economics, and even rides on the twin rails of boundaryless technology and culture. Work sub-cultures (lawyers, educators, entertainers, financiers, etc.) are distinct at some level, partly because the "rules of the game" are different in each segment.

I believe that the fastest growing segment in the world is not a geo-political or traditionally ethnic group, but what I call the Global Business Consumer. These are a people who daily join the swelling ranks of the business tribe. Their scope is global, their culture is "Business 2.0" and their behavioral patterns are consumer-like. In order to reach the Global Business Consumer we need to be living among them and, ideally, part of their tribe. Mission organizations who try to start businesses in order to sneak into the tribe may not be effective.

> *Their location is global. The word "globalization" is not academic for them, but it is a force that has already given them opportunities to work globally, without regard to physical location. They answer phones for Lufthansa from Cape Town. They handle technical support for Cisco from Hyderabad, and they trouble shoot washing machines in the Mid-West from who knows where. They do graphics on websites for companies in San Jose, California from Manila. They partner with Swedes on software development from Chennai. They provide medical diagnoses on patients in Dubai from New York. Their work is global, their competitors are global, their colleagues are global, and while the toppings on their pizza vary, they often eat global, even when local. They are comfortable in airports and on teleconferences. Their characteristics are global.*

> *Their culture, however, is Business. You might want to call it Business 2.0, for the moment, but it will be business of whatever version happens next because they adapt quickly. If they don't they know they will become redundant quicker than last week's web searches. They are not primarily English or Dutch or Korean or Indian or Chinese: they are business. They willingly forego their own tribal identity to be proficient members of the new emerging super-tribe: The Global Business Consumer. I was at a wedding in the South of India a few years ago. There were hundreds of people. My host had informed me, since I was making a speech, that I was to wear a traditional Indian kurta, and I complied. Fortunately for me I talked my youngest son and his friend to pull on the "pajamas" with me*

otherwise I may have been the only man there in Indian garb. Some other men wore suits; some wore jackets, but most wore open neck shirts and "business casual" pants. Even among that crowd I spotted some people in particular who were from my tribe. The other day I had a Skype conversation with one of them who lives in Chennai, is technically based in Princeton, NJ, but spends lots of time in London. We remarked how he and I had more in common with each other than he had with his fellow Indians. Why? Because we are part of the Business tribe.

The final descriptor of this people group is that they are Consumers. Note that I am not saying that they are materialistic, although some no doubt are. I am not criticizing their consumption, but I am simply highlighting how they think, and how they make decisions. For a host of reasons I don't have space or time to describe here, the way in which we make major decisions has changed. Corporations used to send out "requests for proposals" or RFPs to decide which new technology to acquire. At home you could decide with an RFP whether you wanted to buy this or that DVD player. Today, however, a rash of information is readily available to you at work and at home, and you can easily make quick and informed decisions about which iPhone to buy.[16]

The third reason for my considering additional spheres is the "critical success factor" question: "If this sphere was removed could the society function in a manner that God intended in today's world?" I have concluded that without the additional three, society will sub-optimize:

- **Law**: Without a judiciary that is separate or independent of government, the temptation for government to creep to the center will be too strong.

- **Capital**: Without a properly defined and discipled capital sector, wealth creation will be stunted. In fact, without the transformation of this sector—what we call **Repurposing Capital**[17]—economies around the world will continue to be at risk.

- **NGOs**: Without understanding, participating in and properly positioning NGOs, a society cannot be transformed.

A final thought on the spheres of society: I do not believe that church is a separate domain, and I do not believe that technology is either. Let me cover church first. Church (in its proper meaning) should be part of every sector of society. Jesus wants there to be a church in every business, every school and every government department. To grasp this we must have a

---

16   Beyond Business as Missions, by Brett Johnson, February 2010 – http://brett.inst.net
17   Repurposing Capital, by Brett Johnson, Indaba Publishing, April 2010

clear understanding of church. I have no concerns about the survival of the church. I am not concerned that the institutional church will disappear, or the mega church, or the home church. Jesus said he would build his church, and he will no doubt do so in many formats. Building his church in many formats is his prerogative.

Having said this, I believe firmly that Jesus wants to establish his church in the marketplace, and in households in every other sphere of society.

> *Does this mean there is no role for people from the "Religion" sphere, as they should rightly be called? Not at all! We who are kingdom people have a passport to move freely between the spheres. We can speak truth, we can encourage, we can equip. We must recognize, however, that God will raise up apostles, prophets, evangelists, teachers and pastors from within the marketplace to get the job done. Of course they will be in relationship with the rest of the Body of Christ. But they will live there, 24x7, in the world of business making sure that there is a viable expression of the kingdom of God in every business. Doctors and nurses will do the same in hospitals, planting churches in wards. Educators will do the same in schools and universities, planting churches in classrooms and lunch rooms and libraries. Media people will do the same and we will send them emails, "To the church that meets on the movie set in Hollywood..." The TV sitcom "The Office" will get renamed, "The real church."*[18]

Likewise, enabling technologies such as the Internet cut across all spheres of society. Technology is not a subset of business. If you read the book called **I-Operations: How the Internet can transform your Operating Model**[19] you will find a more detailed treatment of this topic. Technology is no more a sphere of society than plumbing or roofing or vinyl siding.

---

18 Beyond Business as Missions, ibid

19 I-Operations: How the Internet can transform your Operating Model, Daichendt and Johnson, Indaba Publishing, 2002

The 10 molehills explained

I do not believe there is anything sacred about one list of spheres of society over another. The 10 that we use at The Institute are useful to us, and may spur your thinking. It is not the purpose of this book to make a case for a particular list of societal sectors. Even though we have good reason for believing these ten are important, there is nothing magical about them, and if you want to group, un-group or segment, feel free to go ahead and do so. Having said that, I will try to explain the ten I have chosen and give a little rationale for each sphere.

Sphere	Rationale
1. Business	The opportunities for business as a platform for ministry are unprecedented. Other spheres are looking to business for answers and seeking to collaborate with business on items such as healthcare, education, law enforcement, and government. Business is a door-opener to the remaining spheres. In our definition, business includes the commercial application of technology.
2. Capital	While capital is in some ways just a resource, the workings of capital markets, financing arrangements and funding models are very different from the everyday workings of Business. While uniqueness is not enough of a reason in and of itself to make it a separate sphere, failure to see the differentiation between running a business and financing a venture often locks corporations in a non-growth mode. Further, the ownership and control issues around capital are significant and need to be understood if they are to be changed. Finally, Capital is more than just the Financial Services sector or industry; it is a world that has far reaching consequences across all of society, as the recent financial crisis has shown. It needs to get back to God's intended purpose if it is to be a positive influence in society.
3. Education	The needs and role of education warrant that it be a separate sphere. How we educate children and adults directly affects their ability to participate in an increasingly knowledge-based economy. Economic pressures in developed and developing nations are making the "elders" of this sphere receptive to business.
4. Family	As the family goes, so goes society. The family is under both obvious and subtle attack on many fronts, and there is even a blurring of lines between business and family. We must look at Family specifically if we are to transform societies.
5. Government	The role of government has strayed far from the biblical intent. Much work has to be done to understand and influence this crucial area. Government, like family, is established by God, and it needs to be reconciled to his ways.

Sphere	Rationale
6. NGOs	Not every country has NGOs. There are, however, still agencies handling what one might call social services. Issues of land management, the environment, social services, etc. need to be considered carefully.
7. Religion	The Religion-sphere has unique needs, a specific sub-culture, and a desperate need for continuous renewal; as such it must be specifically delineated as one of the 10 spheres. Not every community has a church, but all have religion. Some see the Church (universal) as the center of all spheres. We see it two ways: first, as part of the Religion sphere that forms part of the big picture, and second, as part of every sphere.
8. Life Sciences and Healthcare	The move into biotechnology and genomic-based healthcare makes this an increasingly important sphere. Taken together with the fact that many of the challenges of the 21st Century (such as AIDS) are healthcare related, this is a sphere that must be addressed diligently. The ethical issues in this sphere demand that believers be active in bringing a godly perspective to the table.
9. Law	The apparatus of the law is often intricate and is therefore avoided by many people. Properly bounded and practiced, a healthy legal system is crucial to the discipling of a nation. When God discipled the nation of Israel when it came out of Egypt, he used the domain of law as one of his instruments.
10. Media & Communication	This sphere is a major influencer of society and a shaper of culture. It also shapes believers more than we admit. To disciple a nation and transform a society, we must ingrain ourselves strategically in the media industry, and change it from the inside out.

How does one delineate a sphere, sector, domain, mountain, or molehill?

Some will claim their revelation of spheres came from God. Others will claim theirs comes from research, and still others will draw their list from scripture. As indicated earlier, the only seven-mountain reference in scripture is the negative one in Revelation 17:

> [8] The beast, which you saw, once was, now is not, and will come up out of the Abyss and go to his destruction. The inhabitants of the earth whose names have not been written in the book of life from the creation of the world will be astonished when they see the beast, because he once was, now is not, and yet will come.

[9] This calls for a mind with wisdom. The seven heads are seven hills on which the woman sits.[10] They are also seven kings. Five have fallen, one is, the other has not yet come; but when he does come, he must remain for a little while.

This, in and of itself, does not make the seven mountain theory wrong. Still others will determine their spheres based on an analysis of society. Others will use standard industry sectors. Yet others will go with what they call common sense. If we claim our spheres come from revelation, what happened to the revelation of Kuijper, Zacharias, Schaeffer—were they wrong? And how is it that the lists have morphed? Was Kuijper's list of four meant to be the end of it, or was it fine for Bright and Cunningham to add three more? If so, why not re-look at the list today and ask, "What has changed? What are the crucial, indispensable elements of society today?"

Where does the church fit into this?

Everywhere. Just to reiterate, the reality is that the Church, in its true form, fits into every facet of society. I have no concerns about the future of the Church, even though local churches will come and go, and the format of church will surely change over time. Why am I not concerned? Because Jesus said, "I will build my church" and I presume he still means to do that. He told us to preach the kingdom, not the church. We have preached the church and ignored the kingdom. If, however, we actively figure out how to preach the kingdom in every sphere—not to every sphere—then Jesus will build his church there. So, if we live out truth authentically in government, he will build his church there. But if we set church aside as a domain or sphere it becomes an isolated fortress. Then we stay in our high tower and shoot arrows at the other spheres from our citadel rather than go and live among the inhabitants of the spheres, learn their world, love them, and be salt and light among them.

We cannot go as an expert from the world of "church" and think we can lord it over people in the world outside the church. In times past people might have deferred to church leaders because of their superior grasp on spirituality. Today people don't buy this. If they care about spirituality it is because they think that they are already spiritual. Being a "pastor" does not get you extra credit in the different spheres of society, except perhaps Religion, unless you are of the 'wrong' religion for that country.

God is the Glory of every sphere. While it is true that God Himself places a high priority on his Church (meaning, the Church universal, not necessarily the one on the corner), he does not want anything—even a local church—to take preeminence over him. Psalm 106:20 says, "They exchanged their Glory for an image of a bull, which eats grass." Of course one thinks of the Business sphere and the stock exchange where the imagery may well apply: we have exchanged the person of God, in all his glory, for the image of a bull. We like bull markets, and we are prone to place our trust in the markets rather than in God. This does not apply just to Business, however. People in every sphere have a tendency to "exchange their Glory for an image"—the image just varies by sector. If you are a church person, God no more wants to play second fiddle to your church growth strategies or your large sanctuary (if that is where you are placing your trust) than he wants to be second to the bull of Wall Street. He doesn't want the molehills to become mountains. He is, in the first and final analysis, simply far above all. And this includes the industry, if you like, of church.

Scrapping "Business as Missions"

The evolving movement that goes by many names, including Business as Missions (BAM) is in danger of being corralled and relegated to a small sheep pen inside the traditional church farm. This is counter-productive. The intentions are, for the most part good. Well-meaning missions organizations are starting BAM divisions hoping to teach missionaries and others to use business to get the job done.

Business as Missions can be very effective in exploring new ways to build the kingdom. We can limit the effectiveness of the movement, if it is a movement, if we create groups outside of the Business sphere that then have to try to break into the marketplace to transform it. Let me express it differently: there are BAM groups that are intent on doing traditional missions through business, but have no vision for transforming the world of business and work. Work is a means to a missional end, rather than being valuable in and of itself. The marketplace is a cover, not a calling.

The heart of the marketplace movement should be the equipping, commissioning and releasing of people who already work in the marketplace to use their organizations to expand the kingdom in their spheres. One way to help this happen could be to scrap the term "Business as Missions." It is redundant anyway, since the Hebrew word (*avodah*) for business and ministry is the same.

Having said this, I think there is still a role for not-for-profits to play in the marketplace. Those who do not have to earn their keep from the business sphere can be helpful in fostering collaboration, specifically because they are not shackled to the bottom line. If a pastor, for example, has a heart for businesses in his community (because he is seeking the welfare of his city, just as Nehemiah did) he may well encourage business owners to collaborate to create jobs. He is less concerned about competition than they are, and may more readily see collaborative opportunities. As someone has said, "Inside the goldfish bowl is not the best vantage point from which to view the fish."

The flip side of this is that, when mission or church organizations get into 'business' offering free coaching and training for 'business as missions' —or if they do free consulting for companies in the marketplace—they undercut, if not neuter, those who work in the market that they claim to serve. This is a tough issue with no simple answers, but we should at least be aware of the potential challenges.

Why "parachurch" is outdated

Every now and then one hears the term "parachurch" and it is often expressed by those inside a local church. It was somewhat the term to use to describe Christian organizations that were not local churches. Technically the term is fine, because according to Wikipedia, it simply describes "Christian faith-based organizations which work outside of and across denominations to engage in social welfare and evangelism, usually independent of church oversight. These bodies can be businesses, non-profit corporations, or private associations.

Most parachurch organizations, at least those which are normally called parachurch, are Protestant and Evangelical. Some of these organizations cater to a defined spectrum among evangelical beliefs, but most are self-consciously interdenominational and many are ecumenical."

On paper it does not look too bad, but historically it was used in a way that sounded like "not quite as legitimate as real church." Jerry White makes the point, "Struggles over structure, authority, and organizational rights can do nothing but repulse the onlooking world and diminish the effectiveness of the body of Christ."[20] It is time for these struggles to end as we recognize a broad definition of "church" as being essential to tackling all spheres of society. When we focus on the kingdom of God then Jesus builds his church. When we focus on building the local church or a "parachurch" organization, we can become territorial, inwardly focused, and in a us-versus-us mind-set.

If we are to transform society and all of its spheres then we must be thinking kingdom, and not church and para-church. I like what one businessperson in Johannesburg said to me: "The church is a para-business organization." The joke is not far from the truth since "church"

20   The Church & the Parachurch: An Uneasy Marriage, by Jerry White

is not a sphere, but should be infused in all spheres, coming alongside them to bring them into alignment with the One who has rightful dominion there.

Spheres are launching pads not life sentences

One of the tendencies I have observed is that people who profess to be from one domain lock out others who are not from that domain. It is asinine, really, to see businesspeople block out pastors because the latter do not have business degrees, or pastors shut out input from businesspeople because they don't want the church to become a business. If the Church is not the Father's business, whose business is it?

This is not true in all nations. While working with leading government, church and business officers in an African country I learned that all politicians have a spiritual guide or confidante. Often businesspeople are pastors, or government leaders are pastors. When I was in the Ukraine in 1992 I asked the head of a major denomination, "What percentage of your pastors work in business?" His reply surprised me: "99.9%."

God is free to change his mind about which sphere you are assigned to. If he gives you a post in business for a while, do the job. If he transfers you into a job in the Religion sector for a while, take the transfer. And if he leads you into Government, take his lead. It does not matter whose name is on the paycheck (if there is a paycheck) but whose name is on the work order. When you became a follower of Jesus you surrendered your passport. You are no longer just a businessman; you are a kingdom man. You are no longer just an anchor woman; you are a kingdom spokesperson. Don't glory in your molehill, but rather revel in the God of glory who has established the mountain of the Lord as chief among the hills.

If you have to keep changing hats

Having established that God can assign you wherever he wants, there is a corollary, and it has to do with struggling to make the switch between various spheres. You can spot molehill people quite easily. They are the ones who often have to change hats depending on what context they find themselves in. At a conference they are Mr. Speaker, at a church they are Pastor, in the office they are CEO and on the School Board they are Treasurer. If, internally, you become a different person when changing hats you are probably not living an integrated life. If you feel you only have authority in one sphere, then you may be in danger of being a molehill person instead of a mountain person. You may be thinking, "But doesn't Romans 12:3 say that we should not think too highly of ourselves?" True.

We must function according to the measure of faith that we have received, or that has grown in us. But we must not accept parameters on our faith that preclude us from being effective in any facet of life. Beware of thinking that leaves you on the plains. "The Mountain of the Lord will be chief among the hills." You were born to be a mountain person.

In this section

Distinguish spheres from assets

Nehemiah's Public Private Partnership

Part 2

Assets of Society

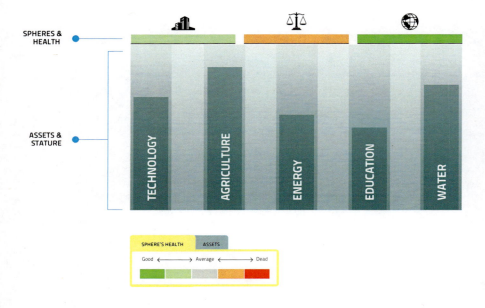

Figure 4: An agrarian economy has well-developed assets of agriculture and water. In this illustration, energy and a critical mass of educated people are lagging. A combination of asset-building and sphere-repurposing is needed to transform society.

Distinguish spheres from assets

One of the challenges in determining the sectors of society could be addressed if we correctly delineated the *assets* of a society from the *spheres* of a society. Every community has assets; every one has some form of capital. Why? Because God is just, and he gives all of us something to work with. There are many forms of capital such as:

- Intellectual
- Relational, familial, tribal
- Governmental/political
- Financial
- Spiritual
- Environmental , etc.

Some years ago we were working in a township in Africa that had about 50% unemployment, poor housing and bad infrastructure. We took a group of high school students and had them brainstorm the needs of the community, and its assets. They then brainstormed creative ways to address the needs. We started a competition to see which students could develop the best business plans for initiatives that may address the community's needs.

At the other end of the social spectrum I sat with the mayor of a small city in the USA recently and asked him, "What are the assets of your community?" He listed them, some tangible and some intangible. We then brainstormed ways to re-brand the city based on their current and emerging assets.

Delineating assets (versus sectors) is useful in the discussion concerning how to shape a city or nation. Some tackle the issues in a society by starting with the pain points, the needs. Others start by looking at the assets. Both are valid, but if we focus on needs without any consideration of assets, then we demean the people in the community, and we fail to see through the lens of possibility. It is not my intent to be too specific about the assets of society, and there is a correlation between assets and spheres.

For example, Education is a sphere of society, and it would be hard to achieve sustained long term transformation without aligning Education to truth. An educated populace, however, is an asset, a key building block for society. Look at the number of graduates in India and the impact an educated populace is having on economic growth.

Look at another example: Law is a sphere of society. But you can have a theoretical legal structure without the rule of law. Take a country like South Africa, for example, where little is done about "petty crime" such as robbery, often accompanied by murder. The statute books are not the problem, but the application is an issue.

Assets vary greatly by geography and culture. What you have in a village in the Amazon will be very different from a suburb in Canada or a barrio in Mexico City. You do not have to be a rocket scientist to grasp the fact that richer countries are happier than poorer ones; this is confirmed in surveys by both Pew and Gallup.

An illustrative list of the Assets of Society could include:

ASSET	WHY IT IS AN ASSET
Land	There are numerous indicators of land quality, arable land, inputs versus outputs and more. In rare instances, there are wealthy nations with little land. In most cases, however, arable land used productively is an asset.
Clean water	Many countries have an abundance of water, but it is not always potable. Water is a scarce national asset that has to be stewarded.
Educated populace	There is a correlation between Gross Domestic Product (GDP) and education levels. Increased education improves the economic and life outlook for citizens and nations.
Electricity	Electricity, in its various forms, is often regarded as a national asset, and for good reason. A consistent, reliable source of electricity is essential.
Ethics	GDP is linked to many factors, and one of them is Ethics. The Corruption Perception Index clearly indicates that nations with low ethics have poor prospects.
Environment	Regardless of your views on global warming, the fact is that a nation's environment can be a major asset that improves quality of life, spawns eco-tourism, and contributes to the national well-being... if it is stewarded.
Technology	Technology is not a sphere of society, but it is an asset. The digital divide—the separation of the digital haves and have nots—is real. Improving access to Internet-related assets in crucial since we live in an era intertwined with information. You may be thinking, 'Well, in rural India people don't care if they have Internet access.' The fact of the matter is that even people in developing nations benefit greatly from being connected. Education, healthcare, law, business, capital... the Internet is an enabling technology for all spheres of society.

ASSET	WHY IT IS AN ASSET
Rule of Law	Nations and citizens benefit from the Rule of Law. The correlation between income and the Rule of Law Index is sometimes know as The Development Dividend.
Mineral resources	Mineral resources can be a two-edged sword, particularly if a nation places reliance on a single mineral. This can lead to laziness and a failure to develop other assets.
Property rights	Having mentioned the Environment as an asset, this should not be at the expense of property rights, which are a cornerstone of economic development. Promote the care of the environment, of course, but be aware that some will abuse a rightful concern and use it to undermine the rights of citizens to own property.
Transportation • Air • Sea • Rail • Road • Water	Producing goods and services, having minerals, possessing arable land... all of these are of limited value if there is no cost-efficient way to get goods and services to market. Transportation infrastructure is another important national asset.

There are other assets, of course. The point is that if we are to be effective in blessing nations then we must understand assets. In fact, every society needs to understand its historical and future assets. I draw a distinction between the two because what was your asset in the past may become your liability in the future unless you adapt to current conditions. National leaders need to pay particular attention to this dynamic. As we consider the discipling of nations we need to work on a two-pronged approach of discipling spheres while building assets. If we lose sight of the opportunity to build assets—and then steward them—we will confuse assets and spheres, and miss investment opportunities that carry with them discipling possibilities. I will cover this later in the section on Public Private Partnerships.

You will have gathered from the table that many of the assets can be two-edged swords; they can used, or abused. That is why we must understand the Genesis 2 mandate to serve, steward and manage.

Nehemiah's Public Private Partnership

By now you must be wondering, "But how does mountain-influences-molehills stuff really work?" Nehemiah sheds some light on the subject that, I believe, could still be very relevant today. I recently listened to a preacher speaking from the book of Nehemiah. He said, "We know, of course, that the primary place of application of these truths today is the local church." Wrong. The book of Nehemiah is about rebuilding a city, not a temple, and not a local church. Ezra had a crack at rebuilding the temple, and we should learn from his experience that rebuilding a church without rebuilding the city in which the church finds itself is not effective. Besides, some scholars think that the two books were once one book, so this should also inform us on the city/church collaboration. This is covered more in my booklet, ***Ashes to Assets***.[21]

I had been on a trip to an African nation and was once again struck by the terrible condition of the infrastructure such as roads, water, electricity, etc. In fact, I watched the local news on TV and as the Minister of Energy announced that a new power plant was imminent, the power went out and he was in darkness... on national television! I then traveled to Spain and saw a contrasting situation. The roads, the transportation, the water, the electricity... it worked! While in Spain I had a dream in which I was speaking to a group of people about rebuilding a city, and telling them "It only takes one man!" Then I woke and the following thoughts came to me from the book of Nehemiah:

- He engaged the construction industry
- Everyone became a builder
- Everyone became a warrior
- There was a plan for the physical reconstruction of the city
- Government approved the plans
- The people built with the intent of creating multi-generational, if not permanent, structure.

I pondered the notion of situations where the actual construction industry and related government entities need to be repurposed in order for a city to be transformed. In Spain, as in many so-called developed nations, the infrastructure within city limits is actually good. The streets are well cared for, there are building codes and standards, formal or informal that have allowed buildings to stand for centuries. Agriculture-wise, there are trees that are over one thousand years old. Water flows, electricity works.

I began asking myself, "Can a city be transformed without the physical look and feel and substance of the city being upgraded?" I know that great public works can flow from revival. I know that reformation evidences itself in the physical. However, ponder with me whether cities in less-developed nations can actually be transformed without a radical, concerted change in what they look like. Without a physical change in the infrastructure:

- People don't see God's order
- They don't have his beauty in front of them

---

21   **Ashes to Assets**, Brett Johnson, © The Institute

Assets of Society 67

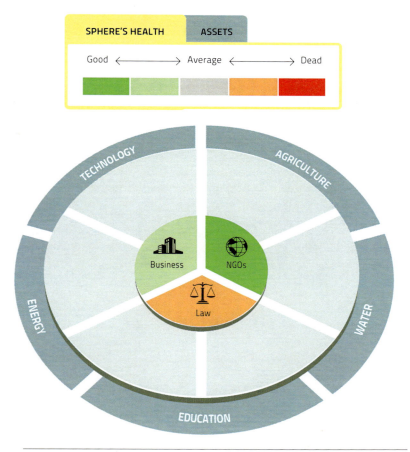

Figure 5: A city where Business, NGOs, and Law are the dominant spheres of society. The NGO sphere is healthy, Business is somewhat healthy, and the Law sphere is weak.

- They easily lose hope because the change that has happened inside is met daily with contradictory evidence in society, such as trash in the streets, potholes, power outages, dirty water, etc.
- The new standards within them are in contrast to the corruption and dismay they live with daily
- They are more easily drawn backwards spiritually
- The cost of business goes up as people have to pay for work-arounds such as their own streets, generators, water purifiers, communications, etc.
- Consumers end up paying more for less

- Entrepreneurship is hampered by lack of infrastructure
- Those with drive and innovation set off for greener pastures where their creative bent is not hampered, OR
- Those with entrepreneurial intent use it for harm and thus corruption becomes commonplace
- Businesspeople are less inclined to pay taxes because they have to carry so many costs themselves.

I wondered if the Nehemiah approach was one of the early forms of what we today would call a Private Public Partnership. Nehemiah had public resources. He had government approvals at the highest levels. Then he challenged the benefiting public to throw in their lot. So, in some senses, the initiative began with an outsider who had government backing, and he then cast the vision and gave the partnering challenge to the private sector who worked, partially at least, with self interest because they built the section of wall in front of their own households. Nehemiah represented a person with hope, who came in from the outside. He also had funding.

What is also interesting is that Nehemiah already had a job: he was careful not to benefit from the rebuilding effort himself. He set a very high ethical standard, and was therefore able to act with moral authority in the situation. No one could say, "Nehemiah is on the take, or he's on a power trip." He was there to do a project, and then go back to his day job.

Then there was also collaboration with the religious sector in that they had to be supportive in order to assure the people that this was part of God's plan. Ezra and Nehemiah were in this thing together. In terms of the sectors of society, we have, so far, five sectors: Government, Capital (which Nehemiah secured before he started), Business, Family and Religion. One could argue that the Legal sector was also involved. (Remember that Ezra had stopped work on the temple because of legal challenges and the related discouragement. Nehemiah had his paperwork at the outset. He had the legal sector taken care of.) The opposition tried to use the Media sector to stop the building, specifically posting public letters. There is no mention of Education per se, but this took place in the temple and in homes, so it would have been a net beneficiary of transformation in the other areas. What we do not have mentioned is Healthcare and NGOs (although, in their case, this was covered by the Religion sector most likely).

What interests me here is the sequence of city-wide transformation because, as people of faith, we tend to start with personal revival and argue that if there is enough spiritual awakening, everything else will be sorted out somehow. The Nehemiah lesson is different. He saw the city was in a shambles, the infrastructure was in disrepair, and people knew little about their spiritual heritage and the promises of God. As long as they were living amidst rubble, it was hard to get them motivated spiritually, so we see, at least with his initiative, a different sequence of things:

1. **Government**—he got the approval from the king.

2. **Capital**—he secured all of the funding that he needed to jump-start the efforts.

3. **Law**—he had letters laying out the clear mandate from the king, and he was ready to deal with opposition.

4. **Business**—he motivated people, in part, by having them rebuild the wall right in front of their homes. In those days, the city-based homes and businesses were often collocated. Therefore, the businesspeople knew that working on the restoration of the city would be good for their business.

5. **Household (Family)**—of course, many had family businesses. However, there was more to it than that: Nehemiah also appealed to their desire to preserve their family lineage for generations to come.

6. **Religion**—the teachers and prophets (Ezra and Haggai) gave fervent support and inspiration and did not insist that people work on the temple (local church) instead of the wall (city) or their business.

7. **Media** was negative in its opposition to building: Tobiah and friends ran an open opposition to Nehemiah. On the positive front the singers and worshipers marched on the city walls as soon as they were rebuilt.

8. **Healthcare**—not covered in the book of Nehemiah.

9. **NGOs**—not mentioned specifically, of course, as these were subsumed by Religion in times past, but now are a separate sector.

10. **Education**—same situation as NGOs.

The latter three sectors were beneficiaries, it would seem. My point here is simply that we should deliberately plan for the strategic engagement of many sectors of society if we are to see societal transformation. Revival on its own (in the traditional view of get them saved, healed, delivered, passionate about God, etc.) is not enough unless that revival translates to re-formation of all sectors of society. So let us explore the Public Private Partnership (PPPs) idea a bit more.

PPPs are arrangements where people from multiple industries generally form consortiums to get important projects, such as transportation, built more efficiently and quicker. They then manage the asset (such as a bridge or a toll road) even though the governmental entity owns it and sets toll rates. In some cases, the PPP also puts up the funding. Over time, they make their money back in profits, and the taxpayers get their services sooner (and often better) at a lower lifetime cost. In today's economy, it is not only a matter of getting projects done sooner, but getting them done at all.

In Florida, for example, a Spanish-based consortium, ACS Infrastructure Development, has closed a $1.6 billion-plus deal to design, build, finance, operate, and maintain a 10.5-mile reconstructed I-595 connector in Broward County from near the Fort Lauderdale Airport and I-95, going west to the I-75/Sawgrass Expressway interchange. A central feature, right down the middle, is three reversible, electronic time-variable tolled lanes called 595 Express. The state will lease the center express lanes from the consortium and collect the tolls. If the tolls must be raised at some point in the future, that will be done by the state, not the private consortium.[22]

There is a National Council for PPP in the USA, and numerous other examples of PPPs around the world.

- Toll roads in China
- The global PPP for hand washing to save children's lives through sanitation practices.
- There are partnerships for weapons removal, such as collaboration on land mine removal that involves the State Department.
- In Canada, there is the Sea to Sky Highway from Vancouver, BC to Whistler.
- A cotton growing area in India shares a testing facility, owned by a trust, among many entrepreneurs, and The Textiles Committee (representing the government) and the trust (representing the industry) share the profits.
- Chile has an innovative approach to the pricing of PPPs using a Least Present Value of Revenues (LPVR) formula. Toll roads and airport operations have been launched as PPPs using this model.
- Large hospital building initiatives in the UK were a result of Public Financing Initiatives, a form of PPPs.

They work this way: the government provides land, water, or other natural resources. The private partner provides technical and operational expertise, and sometimes capital. The public tends to be end users, and

22   Crosscut.com, Matt Rosenberg, April 1, 2009

the profits are shared between the government and private entities. The asset is returned to the government after a set period, usually decades.

Many Christ-followers are looking for ways to influence nations. Often they work around governments, rather than with them. Where they do focus on business, it tends to be at the micro-enterprise level. While this can be good for the individual small business owners, it seldom leads to citywide transformation. The reality is that many national, state and local governments are looking for capital to address major infrastructure projects. They are open to outside help, particularly when it comes with significant funding, and knowledge transfer. They head off to the World Bank, Dubai Port Authorities, China Railroads, etc. while Christians sit on the sidelines.

How does a PPP help disciple a nation? There is a huge opportunity for kingdom-minded investors, fund managers and project initiators to propose projects to governments, and to build into the specifications of those projects (as a condition of funding) the values, ethics, and outcomes that would result in societal transformation. These could include:

- Hiring and training of local contractors based on biblical principles.

- Transparency of reporting.

- Accurate measurement of benefits.

- Defining of building and other codes.

- Insisting on independent judiciary to handle contracts.

- Biblical dispute resolution.

- Allocating a portion of profits to the poor and needy (the Gleanings Fund concept).

- Careful consideration for the environment and appropriate stewardship of natural resources (versus the outsider tendency to dump bad products on unsuspecting markets).

- Perhaps requiring that the participants in the projects go through the **rēp** process of seeing their businesses repurposed.[23]

- Developing a joint scorecard that has a long term, sustainable, broad ranging set of benefits.

PPPs are not without their detractors. They can be done well, and they can be done poorly. The point is they are one example of projects that can be tackled at a city, state or nation-wide level to have societal impact.

---

23   The Institute has a program whereby businesspeople are trained to repurpose corporations.

In this section

Foundations of a City

The dark side and sunny side of the molehills

Operating Model

Key Performance Indicators

Strongmen, Giants

Glory

Keys to Reconciliation, Alignment

Part 3

Foundations of

Societies

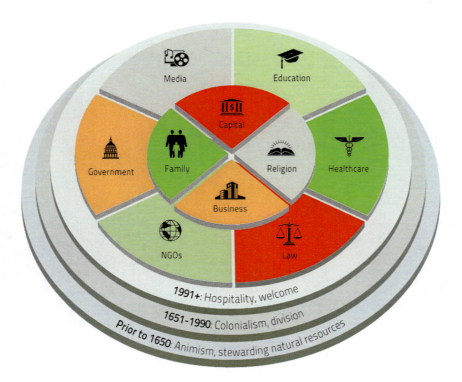

Figure 6: Every city has historical foundations which have a spiritual component. This is an illustration of Cape Town, South Africa, showing a perspective on its foundations. It is known as the Mother City, often birthing things that then move into Africa.

Foundations of a City

In order to see a city, nation or society transformed we need to understand its foundations. If they are good, then we can shore them up. If they were good but are now damaged, our job is to reset them. And if they are bad, we need to raise them up and re-lay solid foundations. This is easier said than done.

> Your people will rebuild the ancient ruins and will raise up the age-old foundations; you will be called Repairer of Broken Walls, Restorer of Streets with Dwellings.[24]

The earlier discussion on the facets of a city will help us to better examine, research and plan action for how to bring the mountain of the Lord to cities and nations.

You might want to start by asking yourself, "What made Jerusalem special?" It was not a city that was designed and built from the ground up according to a plan God had given. (This was true, for example, for the tabernacle.) It was an existing city that God decided would be used for his purposes. It was taken, inhabited and given a God-tweak. What made it special? God chose it, regardless of its past, and he decided to be present there in a special way. Periodically the city was trashed, and when that happened it had to be rebuilt. This involved examining and repairing foundations, walls and gates (to simplify the tale).

Dr. Alistair Petrie does a fine job explaining how we are to research the foundations of cities. "When unholiness goes either undetected or ignored, alternative strongholds invariably become a reality."[25]

En route to Johannesburg, the city where I was born, just before our first **rēp** team was to begin a Venture there, I was reading Isaiah 58 and contemplating the foundations of the city. I asked God to reveal them to me. When we met with the clients on the first day I shared the passage, "they will raise up the age-old foundations." One of our team came to me afterwards and shared that she had recently moved to the city, was praying about where to live, and had a dream about the city. In the dream she saw a map of the greater Johannesburg area, a province called Gauteng. Then the dream changed and under the existing city she saw a dark, but living city which had three pillars: greed, competition and division. There was more to the dream but that information was enough to answer the question about the city's foundations. What did we do with

24   Isaiah 58:12
25   **Releasing Heaven on Earth**, Dr. Alistair Petrie, Chosen Books

the information? We did not call a prayer meeting—intercessors had been praying for the city for decades, and continue to do so. Our work was to get business leaders to formulate practical strategies that would take aim at those three giants, taking them down, and then setting to work in repairing the broken foundations. "This is spiritual warfare" remarked one of our team leaders.

Some years passed and we felt we were still scratching the surface of dealing with the matter of foundations. This time we decided to tackle greed (an expression of Mammon) head on. To do this I researched God's alternate principles, formulated the Kingdom Economics Forum, and then our team taught it in a large house in Johannesburg previously owned by the Chairman of the Chamber of Mines. It was an amazing day. Are we done fixing the foundations? Not yet. But we at least know what our assignment is.

Tackling the sectors in society without addressing the age old foundations is not very helpful. Tending the fruit without examining the root is not enough. We need fresh wisdom to discern the historical roots of cities and nations.

The dark side and sunny side of the molehills

Having become more familiar with facets of society, it may be useful to understand various aspects of each sphere, namely:

- The Operating Model—how it works
- The measures of success, from a traditional and a biblical perspective. These can be called key performance indicators (KPI).
- The Strongmen—the mindsets and forces that are at work in this sphere
- The glory—the potential that the sphere has to represent the nature, character, ways and intentions of God.
- Keys to reconciliation—how to come in an opposite spirit to that which dominates the particular space.

The intent here is not to provide an analysis of each sphere, but just to lay out some thinking tools so that we can better understand any sector of society.

Operating Model

Those reading this from a church background can think of the Operating Model (OM) of the organization as its wineskin. A wineskin was the mechanism that conveyed the wine from the source to its end user, and may have been part of the means of production prior to bottles and barrels. For businesspeople the Operating Model is how an organization designs, develops, markets and manages its goods and services. I cover this in detail in my book, **I-Operations**, and in a paper called *Wineskins*.

The concept of an Operating Model is important because, even though it is generically the same, it changes for every major sector. And in order to transform a sector we need to understand the Operating Model. Jesus was pretty clear about what he came to do: reveal the Father's business. In John 15:15 he made a startling statement which I am paraphrasing to read, "If you don't understand my Father's business you are not my friend." The Father has a business; in our rēp training we teach people the business model of the Father, then seek to reconcile other businesses or organizations to this model. We don't start with the industry best practices and then try to sprinkle some God on these customs.

It is my contention that the nature of the Operating Model is different enough across the 10 spheres that we actually have to think through each one carefully in order to be best equipped to disciple it. In this book I am giving just a glimpse of each sphere so that we can contemplate the task that lies before us as ministers of reconciliation.

Key Performance Indicators

The way we measure success often determines our actions. Our challenge is that we have become inculcated with the wrong measures of success. We have to reconsider what success looks like in each sphere of society, and not necessarily drape the measurements in traditional religious language. Our words can be a barrier to our progress because they narrow our thinking about true discipleship and transformation. The right KPI's can help. The teaching of Jesus in the "sermon on the mount" was an interesting lesson on reshaping measures of success. "You have heard it said... but I say..." In today's language, for example, we might do well to hear, "You have heard it said, 'The bottom line is the bottom line,' but I say, 'The bottom line is obedience to the Father.'"

Strongmen, Giants

We will never transform a sphere if we are enamoured with the giants that live there. As a race car driver told me recently, you turn into what you look at. (This is not good English, but you get the idea. If you focus on the wall, you will crash. If you focus on the track you will be fine.) I don't recommend that we get preoccupied with giants, but it is useful to give thought as to the likely moles we will encounter on the different molehills. Richard Gazowsky put it this way.

> As I meet with prayer leaders, I am amazed at how much effort is put into researching what to pray for. Why research evil or what satan is doing in the earth? I have found it is better for me to spend intimate time with God trying to discover what He wants and desires. As I achieved this intimacy with the Lord, my adventure in knowing Him really took off. The purpose of my prayer life was to teach me obedience and in obeying, I discovered intimacy that has shown me the character of God. Believe me, He is a whole lot more fun than people may think.[26]

We know that we "wrestle not against flesh and blood but against principalities and powers." So when we consider the issues in each sector we are not just talking about credit crunches and job shortages and other things we can see with our natural eyes. At the same time, we remember that we are "seated in heavenly places with Christ Jesus" so our view of the molehills is from a high place, not from ground zero.

Glory

There is another thing we need to understand for each sector or sphere if we are to experience true transformation, and it is the glory of God. The term is not well understood and has become a euphemism for fuzzy, feel good stuff that happens at Christian meetings. The reality is far from this. Being focused on seeing the glory of God in any facet of life is the ultimate aligning principle that will bring that aspect of life into agreement with the Father. Let me state it another way: when we are solely focused on seeing the attributes, the nature, the ways, the character, the goodness of God expressed to the full, then and only then, will we (and all aspects of life) truly be what God intended us/it to be.

Another way to think about the mountain of the Lord is that it is about the glory of God. It is not something on God's agenda, but it is about God being preeminent. It is not about God conquering some aspect of society, but about society realizing that God is far above all. The mountain of the Lord is the capstone and the spheres of society are supporting pillars.

At The Institute we have identified drivers of personal and corporate impact.[27] They are helpful, but they only really come alive when we consider what the glory of God looks like in these areas. The same is true for the 10 sectors of society. We can only hope to see them transformed, reformed, discipled when we get a clearer vision of what it would really

26   The Purpose of Prayer is to teach you Obedience, Richard Gazowsky blog, October 2, 2009

27   The 10-F Model® and The 10-P Model® are registered trademarks of The Institute.

look like for the glory of God to be shown consistently in each sphere. I speak to leaders in many cities and ask them, "What will your city look like five years from now when the kingdom has come?" Most have very little clue. The answers are usually about church attendance, people coming to buildings and being in programs, and other organization-centric perspectives. But with a little prodding the imagination comes alive, and we can begin to see what it might look like when a city experiences the continuous glory of God. It has been a privilege to work with companies who are now imagining products that reveal God's glory, advertising that extends his presence, people who carry his favor, profits that are measured in flow-through not store-up. The list goes on. I will introduce the concept of glory in this chapter and attempt to expand on it towards the end of the book.

Keys to Reconciliation, Alignment

We know from our reading of 2 Corinthians 5 that Christ had the specific purpose of reconciling back to himself that which mankind had forfeited in and since the Garden of Eden. This was part of the work at the cross—reconciliation. What we fail to comprehend is the intended extent or scope of this reconciliation. "For God was in Christ reconciling the world [*cosmos*] to himself." Unfortunately we limit the reconciling work of Christ to people, or the Greek word, *ethnos*. But the cosmos, while it includes people, is bigger than people. It means everything. The plan was that the Godhead would use the same people who forfeited their mandate to extend God's government from the garden on out to once again pick up the mantle and become reconcilers.

Our work, then, is to seek out what is on God's mind (even though we can never fully comprehend it) for different parts of society. One day I was pondering why we had not seen answers to the systemic problems in a township outside Cape Town, South Africa, that was wracked with poverty. I sensed God say, "Because my people don't ask the right questions." If we lose sight of the fact that we are ministers of reconciliation, then we will not have our eyes trained to see the plumb line in the Lord's hands.

Let's explore a little what the characteristics of each sector might be.

SPHERE	BUSINESS
Operating Model	Design, Develop, Market/Sell, and Manage products and services. The basic metaphor is one of imagining, building, selling and managing the life of products or services.
Success - Standard	Market share, profitability, sustainability

SPHERE	BUSINESS
Success - Kingdom	Blessing people, revealing the nature of the Father, collaborating with Him in building products that meet genuine needs
Giants	• Greed, building companies for our own ego, products that 'steal, kill or destroy'—using the ability to work as a way to serve ourselves rather than God • Control—entrapping people in work, rather than liberating them through work • Pride—using work to showcase our abilities rather than to serve mankind
Glory	Businesses that are in God's business
Ways to align	Repurposing Business—helping companies to find their true purpose in the context of God's eternal purpose. Then evaluating every facet of the operating model in light of scripture, and creating a game plan to get things into line with that truth.

The next sphere to consider is the little understood world of Capital. For too many years we have equated banking, financial markets, macroeconomics, money supply and financing as simply part of business. This is a problem because this thinking has left us bereft of strategies and solutions at a time when our competition is really turning up the heat. I have covered this in a separate book called **Repurposing Capital** and in the *Kingdom Economics Forum.*[28]

SPHERE	CAPITAL
Operating Model	Amass capital, control access to it, set terms of borrowing, use money to make more money, passive income, focused control of resources
Success - Standard	Massive wealth, control
Success - Kingdom	• Accessing the storehouses of heaven for projects on earth • Measuring flow-through rather than hoarding • Storing up treasure in heaven • Creating wealth without becoming captive to it
Giants	• Mammon, control • Destroying, enslaving people through debt
Glory	Capital as a tool to expand the kingdom of God. God's people skilled in the stewardship of capital
Ways to align	Repurposing Capital™. Completely changing the way to look at economics

28   Repurposing Capital, Brett Johnson, 2010

Government is another sector that has a unique Operating Model. Today some debate the Christian heritage of the USA, for example. Yet quotes such as these underline the fact that God and Government were interlinked in the minds of the framers of the Constitution.

President John Quincy Adams delivered a Fourth of July speech at Newburyport, Massachusetts in 1837:

"Why is it that, next to the birthday of the Savior of the world, your most joyous and most venerated festival returns on this day [the Fourth of July]?" "Is it not that, in the chain of human events, the birthday of the nation is indissolubly linked with the birthday of the Savior? That it forms a leading event in the progress of the Gospel dispensation? Is it not that the Declaration of Independence first organized the social compact on the foundation of the Redeemer's mission upon earth? That it laid the cornerstone of human government upon the first precepts of Christianity"?

At the Constitutional Convention of 1787, James Madison proposed the plan to divide the central government into three branches: a) Judicial, b) Legislative, and c) Executive. He discovered this model of government from the Perfect Governor, as he read Isaiah 33:22.

> For the Lord is our judge,
> the Lord is our lawgiver,
> the Lord is our king;
> He will save us.

The USA's founders understood that the success of a modern republic would require more than a political document like the Constitution. From their study of history, the Founders had learned of the pitfalls of prior republics. They concluded that even the Constitution alone could not curb individual selfishness. They believed virtues were necessary for sustaining the American experiment. Their fervent prayers were an integral part of the birth of the nation. As a testament to this, Samuel Adams declared on August 2, 1776 as other members of the Continental Congress were still signing the *Declaration of Independence:*

We have this day restored the Sovereign to Whom all men ought to be obedient. He reigns in heaven and from the rising to the setting of the sun, let His kingdom come.

To some this may smack of dominionism; to others it is history; to still others these facts speak to deeper Foundational Principles of Government that are not just American, but biblical. A recent report by The Pew Forum titled *Tolerance and Tension: Islam and Christianity in Sub-Saharan Africa* indicates that 60% of the people surveyed want the laws of their nations to be based on biblical or shari'ah law.[29]

SPHERE	GOVERNMENT
Operating Model	Build infrastructure (governance, legal, physical, financial, etc.), help people grow assets that produce income, tax the income and sometimes the assets, spend on programs that serve stakeholders, manage and monitor programs
Success - Standard	Stability, safety, security, progress
Success - Kingdom	Peace, justice, freedom, health, prosperity, self-government
Giants	• Power, control, exploitation, corruption • Exaltation of government above God • Lording it over people, rather than serving people
Glory	Government is an extension of God's government (not in terms of political affiliation, but in terms of the way leaders govern) that frees and blesses people, making it easier for them to succeed without undue dependence on or interference from government.
Ways to align	Repurposing Government™. Unifying politicians and public servants around a higher set of truths that cross party lines and transcend terms in office.

Next I want to cover the area of Law, or an independent judiciary. In the Old Testament there were judges who ruled Israel. God was king, and the judges helped out in disputes where God's people were not managing to live within God's laws. In such cases the judges stepped in. Even after Israel did appoint kings, there were still independent prophets who were not on the government payroll, and who would render God's judgments as the situation called for it. Today, for example, it is very hard to accomplish societal transformation without property rights. You don't get property rights without good laws. And good laws don't stay in place without an independent, reputable, just judiciary. The challenges include no independent, well developed legal system on the one hand, and an overly active, litigious, divisive legal sector on the other. Hence the need to repurpose this sector.

SPHERE	LAW, LEGAL
Operating Model	Interpret law, assist clients seeking to comply with law, represent clients who may have deviated from law, earn fees for service, or success fees for positive (to clients) outcomes
Success - Standard	Reputation, influence, wealth

29 http://pewforum.org/docs/?DocID=515

SPHERE	LAW, LEGAL
Success - Kingdom	Truth, humility, justice, serving the under-served, harmony
Giants	<ul><li>Perversion of justice</li><li>Control and manipulation through the Law</li><li>Condoning wickedness</li><li>Technical correctness, legal compromise</li><li>Taking away rights of citizens, rather than ensuring their freedoms</li><li>Intimidation, driven by the spirit of fear</li><li>Exonerating the wicked while implicating the righteous</li><li>Injustice</li></ul>
Glory	<ul><li>Law as a reflection of the justice and loving advocacy of God</li><li>The spirit of Jesus pervading matters of justice</li><li>Grace abounding, and truth upheld</li><li>The law of the Spirit written on our hearts</li><li>Redemptive justice is the order of the day; rehabilitation and punishment are held in the right tension</li></ul>
Ways to align	Repurposing Law™. Establishing foundational principles for Law that reflect eternal truth and serve the greater good, not the convenient truth or loopholes that serve man

There is a cross-over between sectors. This is not new. What is getting increased recognition, however, is the importance of what some might call Non-Governmental Organizations. Others have even tried to create a new category called Fourth Sector organizations[30] that function at the intersection of public, private and social sectors. A formal definition of an NGO is a "Private sector, voluntary (and usually non-profit and non-sectarian) organization that contributes to, or participates in, cooperation projects, education, training or other humanitarian, progressive, or watchdog activities. Some of them are accredited by the UN, and some collect donations for distribution among disadvantaged or distressed people. Major worldwide NGOs include International Air Transport Association (IATA), International Chamber of Commerce (ICC), International Committee of the Red Cross, International Organization For Standardization (ISO), Transparency International, World Wide Web (W3) Consortium, and World Wildlife Fund (WWF)."[31] A more current list would include The Bill & Melinda Gates Foundation, the One Campaign, World Vision, and Grameen Foundation.

My friend Os Guinness points out that we need to renew the Christian sources of the uniqueness of philanthropy. There is no civilization in history that has a history of giving, caring and reforms like the West. These

30 The Emerging Fourth Sector, Heerad Sabeti and team
31 See Business Dictionary.com

reforms go back to Old Testament and the giving and caring go back to Jesus. The gospel made a radical transformation at three points:

- View of money
- View of giving
- View of caring

It defined everyone as a neighbor, the validity of personal property, the non-reciprocal nature of giving (not giving to get something in return, but because God is our Giver and we reflect his generosity), and freedom from laws and constraints in giving. We need a re-engagement in civil society initiatives.

SPHERE	NGOs
Operating Model	Identify issues, form organizations, recruit adherents/raise supporters, arrange initiatives or programs: some convene, others mobilize, others develop concepts, and others create standards to which the Government and Legal sectors legislate
Success - Standard	Renown, reach, influence, causes implemented
Success - Kingdom	People served, needs met, lives changed
Giants	• Idealism, humanism, misguided altruism • Reliance on man, not God, for answers to human issues
Glory	The compassion of God, the love of God and the truth of God all presented together, and supported by loving action
Ways to align	Highlight how the full truth of God creates a better solution.

When Kuijper expressed the notion of sphere sovereignty he was essentially against one sphere taking over what was rightfully the responsibility of another sphere. We can avoid a lot of problems if we start with the realm of Family first, then see what is left over for the other spheres, including Religion. When families do not understand their role or abdicate their responsibilities then more gets ceded to Government, Education, NGOs, etc. So it is important that we look closely at Family as a sector of every healthy society. Scripture says that God "sets the lonely in families." We set the lonely in institutions—churches included—where they get more lonely. We think we know family, but we have lost its richness and intended scope.

SPHERE	FAMILY
Operating Model	Love, procreate, nurture, equip, build launching-pad under, and release/send out children
Success - Standard	Stable marriages, healthy homes, children reflecting well on parents
Success - Kingdom	Multi-generational walk of faith, taking the expansion of the kingdom of God to new heights in successive generations, stewarding a spiritual legacy
Giants	• Fatherlessness, broken homes, one-generation thinking • Abortion, childlessness. • Elitism, pride of life, discrimination.
Glory	Consistent, multi-generational obedience. Acceptance, love, inter-generational honor
Ways to align	Bring order, develop family calling, instill effective household management, re-prioritize family

One of the areas that has been relentless in its erosion of families is the Media. Fathers are depicted as deadbeats, mothers compete to be sexual predators, kids are lauded for defying authority and small children are the center of the universe. Many movies have the obligatory but unnecessary-to-the-plot gay couple. News is biased, and entertainment has become a megaphone for philosophies of life. Media needs repurposing. (Some cluster Media, Arts, Entertainment and Communications together, and others divide these into different sectors. There is a convergence, thanks to technology, of many media streams, so I call the whole sector Media.)

SPHERE	MEDIA
Operating Model	Ideate, produce, promote, develop secondary products, manage; aggrandize stars, movies, lifestyles, etc. that will, in turn, feed the system.
Success - Standard	Fame, viewers, advertising revenue, wealth
Success - Kingdom	Truth is celebrated, creativity is rampant, people are reflecting God's glory in their person and their work, transparency is the order of the day, and ideology is not twisting opinions.
Giants	• Liberalism, perversion, making "role models" out of perverse people • Idolizing what looks good rather than what is good • Political correctness, tolerance, sensationalism
Glory	Beauty, creativity, hope, communication of truth
Ways to align	Celebrate creativity, exceed worldly levels, develop inspiring content, starve bad media of finances, etc.

A debate is raging in the US—or perhaps a debate should be raging—on the issue of healthcare. It is an area where the worldview of leaders and the medical care of the population and the aims of business and the philosophies of education collide. We have moved so far from "I am the Lord who heals you" that we have lost sight of how this sector should operate. When Government plays wealth-reallocater and when Healthcare plays God we get disastrous results. And when businesses put the bottom line above the wellbeing of individuals, communities and nations we exacerbate the problems. When we ignore the solutions of scripture for the concoctions of man and treat lifestyle issues with pills; when we forsake common sense and replace it with recommended daily allowances... it is time to repurpose healthcare.

SPHERE	HEALTHCARE
Operating Model	Assess, examine, prescribe, fulfill, monitor, manage (illness, wellness, cost)
Success - Standard	Mortality rates, life expectancy, wellness indicators, access to care, quality of care, cost of care. Caregivers serve where it is lucrative.
Success - Kingdom	Blind see, lame walk, deaf hear, dead are raised, disease is reversed, fewer get ill, diseases are eradicated. Caregivers serve where they are called.
Giants	• Mammon—greed before service. Systemic injustice • Determinism, playing God, lack of compassion for people
Glory	People have life, to the full
Ways to align	Understanding the medical system, its strengths and weaknesses. Understanding the biblical approach to Healthcare. Gap analysis. Finding the system-wide transformation triggers. Targeting systemic 'cures' at the system, at organizational and personal levels.

There is a component of Healthcare that relates to Education. Universities, research institutions, and specialized clinics play a large role. Other sectors also intersect with, and sometimes overlap with Healthcare, such as when people get education at their place of work. Governments and NGOs also influence and sometimes control Education. So we turn our focus to this sector of society which must also be repurposed.

Before jumping into the specifics let me remind us that in order to exercise the ministry of reconciliation described in 2 Corinthians chapter 5 we have to be engaged in two realities simultaneously. Without this we cannot pull them into greater alignment. As we look at education forget, for the moment, about "Christian schools" and consider how education broadly can be more aligned with God and his purposes.

Foundations of Societies 87

My friend, Michael Cassidy, speaks of the "Christian origin of the early medieval universities where it was Christ and the Logos doctrine of John's Gospel and the biblical World View which served as the controlling Centre of the academic enterprise, with Theology as the Queen of the Sciences. As Oxford University's motto declared: Dominus Illuminatio Mea, i.e., God My Illumination. If God does not illuminate academia it will operate in darkness, and that, I believe, to be the case now. That was the key to the medieval universities for nearly a thousand years. And it is time it was rediscovered."

SPHERE	EDUCATION
Operating Model	Research, formulate/write, teach.
Success - Standard	Exalting the thinking of man. Shaping the worldview of mankind—one where everything can be explained apart from God. Getting accolades from fellow academics.
Success - Kingdom	Exalting the truth of God, renewing minds, informing a biblical worldview, assisting individuals to achieve their full potential in God.
Giants	• Humanism, egocentrism, ideology • Believing we can think our way out of problems and into salvation
Glory	Seeking, understanding, applying, teaching, imparting Eternal Truth in order to reveal truth-reflected to a pleased Father, and truth-embodied to a needy world.
Ways to align	Seeking out God's ways, his mind, his precepts, his eternal laws, and submission to the Word

So we come to the final sector. Missing, as you will have noted earlier, are two spheres that often appeared in early lists of "mind molders" or mountains, namely, "church" and "missions." Why? Because a society can be found to have religion without church. Also, it does not take long for vibrant church to become organized religion. In an earlier article[32] I observed that it takes about 18 months for the wineskin to go from supple to crusty, and another 18 months to go from crusty to cracked. In other words, we are always only three years away from religion. Given that there are enough denominations, streams or franchises out there, at any point in time society needs religion to be repurposed in order for that society to be transformed.

This is a fairly contrary view to the unspoken view which effectively says, "We have the truth so we don't need to change. In fact, the enlightened will see that our old time religion is good enough. If they don't, they can go to

32 Wineskins, Brett Johnson, Christian Management Report.

hell, because we are not changing our wineskin." Admittedly, this sounds a bit harsh. We religious people do try to adapt, of course, and embrace words like relevance and current and friendly. But changing all facets of the Operating Model (the wineskin) takes a lot more work than podcasting sermons or getting a Facebook account.

Kingdom-minded people are great candidates to be involved in Repurposing Religion™. Why? Because they carry the life of the kingdom within them, and wherever there is an ounce of life it demands a continually renewing wineskin.

SPHERE	RELIGION
Operating Model	The typical OM has these components: • Activities: Love, mend, train, send. • Scope: Jerusalem, Judea, Samaria, Ends of the Earth. • Most of the budget and focus goes into "loving and mending" (bringing in and fixing) people who are pro-church.
Success - Standard	Numbers in attendance, financial stability, sub-culture compliance.
Success - Kingdom	Loving God, loving mankind, finishing the work he gave us to do.
Giants	• Religiousness, disobedience, compromise of truth, packaging God • Sensationalism, stoicism • Complacency, loss of passion for God, making an idol of the mind • Over-spiritualizing while ignoring the Spirit • Self-righteousness • Condoning sin in order to keep control.
Glory	The presence of God manifested in many ways. God himself as our goal, not religious systems. The love of God pervasive, demonstrated in unity, graciousness, focusing on the main things, and compassion. Continuous worship. A church rejuvenated, urgent, focused, abiding, empowered, righteous, pure and joyful.
Ways to align	Hunger, thirst, seeking, receiving revelation, routine overhaul of the OM, getting back on God's agenda... Repurposing Church.

We need people who can assess and repair foundations, modern Nehemiahs, if you like. What additional competencies are needed to transform society?

Foundations of Societies 89

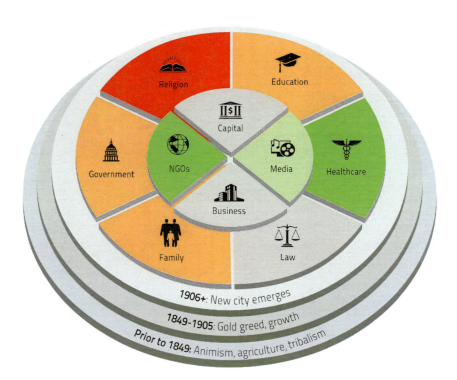

Figure 7: An illustration of the Foundations of San Francisco. While this example is more of a historical sequence, the related spiritual foundations can parallel the major eras of a city.

In this section

Created for unity, marked by division

We prefer to work alone

The work of transformation is bigger than any of us

It takes a network

Households are the keyhole to all sectors

BELTS

Societies are Relational

Business must be defined afresh

Transforming Society requires Repurposing Sectors

Dislodged by difficulty

Impact at the intersection of spheres

Called Corporations

Repurposing Business

Part 4

Competencies Required to Transform Society

Created for unity, marked by division

The Muslim man sitting next to me on the plane was pointed in his comments. While his facts were not specifically accurate, they captured the gist of what many see as unfathomable: "Christians have so many divisions. There are Methodist-Catholics, Baptists, Presbyterians... In Islam, we have one truth."

The Christian world has seen its fair share of squabbles. To insiders the differences may look like nuances, like how much water constitutes a baptism, but to those who don't know a Presbyterian from a vegetarian our divisions don't make much sense. The early disciples struggled to stay united even with Jesus in their midst, and before he left planet earth Jesus prayed urgently for his disciples "that all of them may be one."[33] There are many wonderful leaders and organizations who routinely honor each other, speaking at each other's conferences, and making gifts to each other's work. This is "coming at things in the opposite spirit" at its best. But we still have too many instances of going it alone. Why?

We prefer to work alone

While it is true that unity of spirit is not necessarily unanimity of thinking, and while project-specific efforts are quite common, in general, many groups prefer to work alone, or within their denomination or stream or organization. One of the top reasons why career missionaries leave the mission field is that they cannot get along with other missionaries. We pay lip service to collaboration, but avoid it if we can. When speaking at a conference on technology and the church my friend Mark Kvamme encouraged Christian organizations to "practice promiscuous partnering."

There are numerous reasons for not working together. We are all so busy with our own thing that it is hard to carve out the time to partner. There are differences in approach, focus and doctrine. Specialization makes us stick to our niche. We also can lack the expertise and tools to be effective partners. A lot can get done when we focus on outcomes and not on who gets the credit.

> Not to us, not to us, O Lord,
> but to your name be the glory,
> because of your love and faithfulness.[34]

There is another reason, however, and it is money. If we are brutally honest we will admit that the reason we don't want to work with others is because we are concerned that "our" donors will defect and become "their"

33 John 17:21
34 Psalm 115:1

donors. This is a particularly difficult prospect for those organizations who live on the fundraising treadmill. Mammon does not confine itself to business. We have yet to see what God will do when we care less about who, except him, gets the credit.

The work of transformation is bigger than any of us

It is hard to say what causes transformation. When a city gets transformed we can point to the death of a martyr, unity among church leaders, a significant and public miracle, decades of faithful prayer, or the overthrow of some evil force at work. Or perhaps the work of a major corporation shapes a town, or a political leader arises who experiences personal reformation. With God as the CEO, however, it is likely that he directed many of his subsidiaries to work on different aspects of transformation in a manner that made the outcome more certain. No one organization can take the photos, raise the flag and claim the credit. The work of transforming society is simply bigger than any of us.

It takes a network

Some years ago I began thinking about the breadth of competencies needed to transform a city. Teams from The Institute focus on Repurposing Business® but we know there was more to do, and that we have but a small part to play. I therefore began to consider who were the primary, secondary and emerging organizations or leaders for each competency. I will not take the time to explain why I believe each competency is necessary as they should be fairly intuitive. I have listed the competencies in alphabetical order, not in a logical sequence. By the time you read the table below it will, by definition, be out of date. The point is not to pigeonhole organizations or people but to suggest a framework of thinking so that you can develop your own Impact Network.[35] (My apologies in advance if you find your name here and you have repositioned yourself by the time this gets to print. The organizations illustrated here are those I happen to know, so they are on my radar; the matrix is not exhaustive, but applicable to me. I have used real names, where possible, to make your part, and my part, in transformation practical and personal.)

This idea is not just about a tool or framework of thinking. In recent times the debate has bubbled about whether Business as Missions is a good name for how marketplace people are co-laboring with God. A focus on Business as Missions (or church restoration, or political reform, or revival, for that matter) is too weak a concept to unify a diverse body because it puts the focus on the means, and not the end. The kingdom principle of alignment means having an eye on the glory of God. Stopping short of full societal transformation will inevitably lead to a focus on some subset (prayer, discipling, teaching, trading) and miss God's end goal.

35 **Business Impact Networks**, The Institute booklet www.inst.net

Competencies Required to Transform Society 95

COMPETENCY	PRIMARY	SECONDARY	EMERGING
Capital		Ibex Various Venture Philanthropists	Social Venture Funds
Church planting in businesses			David Watson Ed Silvoso Peter Wagner **rēp**
City Reaching	Ed Silvoso	Graham Power/ GDOP	Bethel, Bill Johnson
Discipling, Coaching	Crown Financial	Convene Dennis Peacocke CBMC	
Prayer	Global Day of Prayer IHOP		24x7
Prophetic	Chuck Pierce Elijah List crowd Bob Jones et al		
Mobilization	Mega churches Large mission agencies	Ed Silvoso	Priority Associates Call2All/Business, Al Caperna
Repurposing Business	The Institute / **rēp**		
Research, Strategic Thinking	Alistair Petrie George Otis, Jr.	The Institute / **rēp**	
Publishing	Zondervan et al Giant Partners	Os Hillman Dennis Peacocke Ed Silvoso Inside Work, Al Lunsford	Justin Foreman (BAM blog)
Sphere-specific Transformation		ICCC	**rēp**
Teaching	Dennis Peacocke Os Hillman Peter Wagner Landa Cope	Ed Silvoso ICCC Regent University The Institute /**rēp**	Rich Marshall
Trade, Doing Business	Gunnar Olson-ICCC Dwight Nordstrom	Ken Eldred Paul Tan	Traditional missions doing "tent making"

Table: The Transformation Impact Network Competencies Matrix. An illustration of the competencies required to transform society.

Households are the keyhole to all sectors

Since 2003 my team and I have grown tremendously in our appreciation of households. Part of this understanding comes from our study of the inter-connectedness of businesses, households and churches in scripture. A quick reading of the book of Acts reveals three instances when an entire household came into relationship with God. Personally, I had viewed these as a freak occurrence of the New Testament. Reading more carefully I see that these were not isolated incidents.

We can start a study of household with Cornelius because he was specifically told by an angel that if he sent some employees down to another town and they brought back a man named Peter, then Peter would explain to Cornelius how he could get saved. The angel added this twist, "you and all your household."[36] So Cornelius crammed the living room with people and, true to what the angel said, they all came to know Jesus, were filled with the Spirit, spoke in other tongues, and were baptized. They got the whole package.

Read on and you see a similar outcome with a businesswomen and her employees as Lydia and her whole household also were "saved" all at once.[37] Keep going in the book of Acts and you will come across the law enforcement man who was running the prison, there was "a sign and a wonder" when the prison shook, and this created an opening for Paul to explain what was going on. The jailer and his whole household believed. Acts 16 puts it this way:

> [29] The jailer called for lights, rushed in and fell trembling before Paul and Silas. [30] He then brought them out and asked, "Sirs, what must I do to be saved?"
>
> [31] They replied, "Believe in the Lord Jesus, and you will be saved—you and your household." [32] Then they spoke the word of the Lord to him and to all the others in his house. [33] At that hour of the night the jailer took them and washed their wounds; then immediately he and all his family were baptized. [34] The jailer brought them into his house and set a meal before them; he was filled with joy because he had come to believe in God—he and his whole family.[38]

36   Acts 11:14
37   Acts 16:15
38   Acts 16

There is yet another example of this phenomenon.

> Crispus, the synagogue ruler, and his entire household believed in the Lord; and many of the Corinthians who heard him believed and were baptized.[39]

After I read these four accounts I became curious. How many times does scripture speak about household? After all, only once did Jesus say, "you must be born again" and yet I believed that this is enough. In the book of Acts I see a whole company of people being born again, three or four times! How pervasive is this idea?

First, a word search reveals 162 references to household in scripture. You will find related examples, such as Noah building an ark "for the salvation of his house." Remember that the ark is a picture of Jesus. Could it be that Noah set a precedent for a whole family getting saved at once? Then we get to Abraham, where God made a covenant with Abraham and his whole household.[40] All of the them received both the mark and the benefits of the covenant that God made with their boss, Abraham.

> *A focus on Business as Missions (or church restoration, or political reform, or revival, for that matter) is too weak a concept to unify a diverse body because it puts the focus on the means, and not the end.*
>
> Brett Johnson

All of the Old Testament examples confirmed what I see in the book of Acts. So I thought, "Surely Jesus would have addressed the matter if it is this important." We all know that the first miracle Jesus performed was turning water into wine, thereby revealing his glory. The second miracle Jesus did resulted in salvation coming to a whole household.

> Then the father realized that this was the exact time at which Jesus had said to him, 'Your son will live.' So he and all his household believed. This was the second miraculous sign that Jesus performed, having come from Judea to Galilee.[41]

39   Acts 18:8
40   Genesis 12
41   John 4:53-54

You will remember Jesus' encounter with Zacchaeus where he observed the taxman's repentance and said, "Today salvation has come to this house." Twice Jesus affirmed that salvation came to a house. Why do I go line fishing when Jesus went net fishing?

Taking the concept a little further, the word economics comes from *oikos*, and means household management. We have tended to drive a wedge between work and faith, but economics derives from a church word, and church (*ekklesia*) derives from a political term for a group of called-out people. The Church is referred to as the household of God [42] and God had no problem making effective household management a prerequisite to biblical leadership.

> A deacon must be the husband of but one wife and must manage his children and his household well. [43]

One evening we were attending a service at Bethel Church in Redding, California. Artists were painting as the worship progressed. A young woman painted a scene where a giant key was unlocking the planet earth. Surrounding the key were houses. It was a reminder to me that households are the key to unlocking all spheres of society, whether these households are literal homes, or families, or businesses, or households of faith (what we call churches).

There are households in all spheres of society. The jailer was in law enforcement, Lydia was in business, the synagogue leader was from the Religion sphere, Zack was in the IRS, Noah (who built an ark for the salvation of his house) wasn't really a ship builder, just one obedient man... read the ends of Paul's letters and you will see how prominently household played into the fabric of the church.

Household is also key to the extension of the kingdom. We spend too much time wondering about where the harvest is ripe. In Luke 10 Jesus tells us not once or twice or three times, but five times. House, house, house, house, and house!

> [5] "When you enter a **house**, first say, 'Peace to this **house**.' [6] If a man of peace is there, your peace will rest on him; if not, it will return to you. [7] Stay in that **house**, eating and drinking whatever they give you, for the worker deserves his wages. Do not move around from **house** to **house**." [44]

---

42 1 Timothy 3:15
43 1 Timothy 3:12
44 Luke 10:5-7

Many speak about working where God is working. He was back then, and still is, working in houses—houses of prayer, houses of business, houses of education, houses of government... anywhere there is a head of a household. Jesus went on to give some clues about how to approach heads of households or men/women of peace. (Lydia was, as a reminder, a woman of peace who was head of her household.)

BELTS

How, then, can we undo some of our evangelistic, religious trappings and approach everyday heads of households such as CEOs and members of parliament? The acronym BELTS can be a handy reminder about a practical thing you can do when you next walk into your favorite coffee shop or hardware store.

Bless the household. Say, "Peace to this house..." but try to say it in modern English. "Good day... I trust things are going well... I love your business and am rooting for you in this economy. May you have great favor today." (You will need to adjust your language to your context, but learn to speak out blessing in creative, non-religious ways.)

Eat with them. "Eat whatever is set in front of you." I am not saying you can't choose your own food when you ask the storekeeper out for lunch, but take the time to get close to him or her. Take your hairdresser a cup of coffee. Share a bagel or a donut or something. Find a way to eat together. Samuel Johnson once said, "Eating lubricates business."

Listen to their needs. Ask good questions, listen for the answers, and identify a point of need. Their need is your opportunity to at least pray. When you take the risk of praying, God loves to step in. When he does so, then people ask, "What is going on?" A friend of mine sat at lunch while a co-worker shared his needs. My friend felt his chest pounding and knew he had to offer to pray for the man who was clearly not a follower of Jesus. To cut a wonderful story short, that weekend God answered the prayers for the impossible. At a staff meeting on the Monday after the weekend the man said, "Hey... if any of you have any problems, ask Ben to pray for you." And he shared his story, or what we would call his testimony. Many people came to Christ in the months that followed, including the head of the department, who became a woman of peace.

Talk with them, sharing the truth about the kingdom of God in the context of relationship and caring. My friend's relationship, attentiveness to a need, followed by the prayer, accompanied by the miracle led to lots of talk. Many more people (32 at last count) came to know Jesus as a result.

Signs and Wonders: Pray for them at their point of need expecting God to show up with the kind of miracle that meets them where they need it most. One of my friends works in a well-known technology company. They were having problems in his division, even considering closing it down. He told his boss, "I am involved with this organization that prays for marketplace miracles; we need a miracle. Will you agree with me if I pray?" The boss (a pre-believer) listened as he prayed, and the business has turned around.

We can implement BELTS in every sphere of society. This is not an evangelistic tool. Jesus did not send the 12 or 72 out to get converts or preach salvation. He sent them with the instruction to preach the kingdom of God, and he gave them pointers as to how to do it.

The idea is not to give us a formula for "conquering" Media, for example, but to remind us that in order to impact Media we need to:

- Go to their place of business, not to judge it but bless it.
- Eat with them.
- Listen to what troubles or delights or interests them.
- Tell them, "the kingdom is here" but not in religious language, and
- Pray for miracles, putting your faith on the line for something that will blow them wide open to the gospel in their context.

Jesus worked along these lines.[45] There was a man named Peter and Jesus got into his business (which was a boat). Peter observed while Jesus gave a pretty good talk to a group of people nearby. When he had finished speaking Jesus said, "Head out a little and toss your net in the water on the other side of the boat." It was as if Jesus was saying, "You heard what I said, now let's make it nice and personal for you in a way you cannot deny in your business." Peter participated, whether he expected a miracle or not. God showed up, and then the fish showed up. Peter realized he was encountering something bigger than himself, out of his depth. He then became aware of his sin, and said, "Out of my boat and out of my life—I am a dirty fisherman." Jesus responded, "I can work with that, but I will need to expand your scope a little and make you a fisher of men." Peter answered, "If you can transform my business in one quick miracle you can probably transform me too, so sign me up!"

Almost every time that we go into a business we ask them, "Where do you need a miracle?" or, "Tell us your biggest point of need because we want to pray for a miracle." Our surveys indicate that 61% of the business

45   Luke 5:1-10 with poetic license

leaders experience a significant miracle within weeks. This is by no means a perfect score, but this is on top of all of the "normal" breakthroughs like restored marriages, inter-generational reconciliation, and people coming to Jesus. God turns the heads of businesspeople when sales cycles drop from 9 months to 45 days, when broadband licences are granted, when businesses are sold, when new housing designs are given in a dream, broken equipment is healed, and a swarm of locusts settles on a crop then leaves again without taking a nibble. God still markets using signs and wonders. Our job is not to hit some percentage or another, but to try to be faithful in serving where people need to see God cares, and going where he told us people are ready: from house, to house, to house. Houses are businesses, they are classrooms, they are coffee shops, and they are families. They are churches too.

The kingdom principle of alignment means having an eye on the glory of God. Stopping short of full societal transformation will inevitably lead to a focus on some subset (prayer, discipling, teaching, trading) and miss God's end goal.

Brett Johnson

Societies are relational

We can slice and dice the spheres of society and miss the fact that societies are relational. They may or may not fall into our neat buckets. It is therefore imperative that we recognize the key relational elements in any community. At The Institute we have grappled with how we can have a positive influence in society while remaining focused on our core competencies. Like you, we cannot do it all. We also recognize that we cannot ignore key relational groups in a city or nation and hope to transform society. Many entities focus, for example, just on the elite. Others ignore the elite and focus on the poor. Each claims a biblical reason for doing so. Others, however, are more holistic and when their service to the poor opens doors to the elite they step through those doors. When they have access to leaders they urge them to remember the poor.

In order to be involved in transforming society there would seem to be at least eight groups we should consider. Using my own business as an example, my colleagues and I need to facilitate work with various relational clusters in order to achieve the transformation of society, or the discipling of nations, a mandate of every believer.

- Men and Women of Peace: Selected leaders who are city elders and influencers.

- Households of peace: Corporations, be they government departments, businesses or churches, with a passion to see transformation begin with them. These are not just the individual leaders, but whole companies committed to transformation. Households of peace become launching pads into many other corporations because they have a draw, an ability to pull others into their transformational slipstream.

- Spheres of society: Key sectors which, when transformed, will cause a tipping point in a city or nation.

- Called Corporations: The foundational businesses that God has allowed to be placed in cities or nations, that determine the ethos, complexion, direction and perhaps calling of cities.

- A critical mass of corporations that are being repurposed (in our case, through **rēp** Ventures, but this can happen in many ways).

- Integrated workers: With a broader set of working people who are living integrated lives and moving towards convergence.

- Broad equipping of a large pool of entrepreneurs who are not mid-sized corporations or called corporations, or households of peace, but for whom the truths with which we have been entrusted still has relevance.

- Core companies: Businesses or entities at the lowest economic levels that provide work-enabled hope for the poorest in society (in the biblical view of work, not just work for work's sake). These are not just micro enterprises, but those that have enough critical mass and momentum to spin off secondary businesses or ventures.

Business must be defined afresh

I asked a young entrepreneur, "How would you define business?" Having graduated top of his class from Harvard University I expected a complex answer, but instead he said, "Buying and selling goods or services." So I asked, "...for a profit?" And he said, "Not necessarily." Many people cannot answer as clearly as this young man because they feel that they have to weave in "the profit motive" whereas he was describing the work and mechanisms of business. Many people of faith struggle with their work and careers because they do not have a biblical definition of business. It stands to reason that if we do not have a proper definition of business, government or education, to name some spheres, we will not be able to transform them because we will be seeking to align them to the wrong template.

The definition of "a company" has shifted in recent times. It came originally from two Italian words, *cum,* or *com*, and *panis*, meaning, "those who gathered around bread." In the industrial age the definition became technical and legal, but today people are apt to talk about the soul and heart of a corporation. Zohar and Marshall introduced the notion of "spiritual capital" where their concept comes the Latin word *spiritus*, which means, "that which gives life or vitality to a system." It was initially contested as be unscientific, but is gaining traction.

Forgive me for being personal, but let me give you an example from my own work. Many years ago one of my colleagues asked me, "Brett, are we a business or a ministry?" I replied, "Yes!" He looked a little quizzical and thought he would re-explain because it was clear to him that I did not understand the question. "You see, Brett, if we are a business then we operate on business principles, but if we are a ministry then we operate as a ministry."

We want to intertwine modus operandi, motives and money to define something. Our motive should always be "to glorify God." Our modus operandi must always be excellence appropriate to the situation and consistent with the character of God, and God should always be the source. Isn't this true whether we run a medical clinic, a library or a factory? Please don't tell me that the answer depends on whether you are a business. In Hebrew the word for work and ministry is the same. Scripture does not allow for schizophrenia.

> *In that day the Branch of the Lord will be beautiful and glorious, and the fruit of the land will be the pride and glory of the survivors in Israel. Those who are left in Zion, who remain in Jerusalem, will be called holy, all who are recorded among the living in Jerusalem. The Lord will wash away the filth of the women of Zion; he will cleanse the bloodstains from Jerusalem by a spirit of judgment and a spirit of fire. Then the Lord will create over all of Mount Zion and over those who assemble there a cloud of smoke by day and a glow of flaming fire by night; over all the glory will be a canopy. It will be a shelter and shade from the heat of the day, and a refuge and hiding place from the storm and rain.*
>
> *Isaiah 4:2-6*

Back to my personal example:

- Our identity statement says The Institute has "The head of a think tank, the hands of a business, and the heart of philanthropy."
- Over the past 13 years, the definition of a company has been in flux, so it bears some revisiting and clarification.

Transforming Society

- We at The Institute are business with a greater purpose. Some people call these new types of companies B Corporations.

  B Corporations are a new type of corporation which uses the power of business to solve social and environmental problems. B Corporations are unlike traditional responsible businesses because they: Meet comprehensive and transparent social and environmental performance standards; Institutionalize stakeholder interests; Build collective voice through the power of a unifying brand.[46]

- We develop and deploy assets in ways that achieve our Purpose, which is a higher purpose, a corporate calling.

- Our corporation creates impact both directly, and by collaborating with others for   greater advantage. Our input draws their input. (This is the law of draw.)

- We need multiple types of work in order to achieve the transformation of society, or the discipling of nations, which is the mandate of every believer. The *direct* work usually is done at market rates, and has a greater margin.

- The partnered work done by people from The Institute can be:

  - At market rates, or

  - At lower rates that could be "free" or a contribution that causes others to give their assets, such as time, money and expertise, and

  - Done in conjunction with volunteers, NGOs, social sector organizations and businesses.

- Where contributions in cash are given, they will generally be given through our partner organizations, and not to or through The Institute as a for-profit entity (from a tax perspective).

There is nothing prohibiting people giving to a business if they believe that the business is accomplishing greater good, societal impact, kingdom impact (or whatever you call it) efficiently. However, people may have trouble understanding this for the foreseeable future.

In other nations we sometimes collaborate with like-minded NGOs/social sector corporations.

- The work (provision of goods and services) will generally be organized using the infrastructure, assets, and leadership of The Institute. The product/service delivery mechanism will still be the business.

---

46   http://www.bcorporation.net/about

- Therefore, our "corporation for greater good" has multiple facets: "The head of a think tank, hands of a business, heart of philanthropy."® The investments we make are designed to be leveraged through the investments of others into societal transformation.

I went on to suggest to my colleagues that we do various things for a season:

1. That we scrap the use of the word "model" because it comes with the baggage of "business model."

2. That we avoid the descriptors "business" and "ministry" when talking about what we do, recognizing that the use of the words "business" and "ministry" are often, unfortunately, counter-productive in our discussions. This is not because we mean it to be so, but because these terms carry historic meaning, so when we use them we have to make assumptions about what the other person is thinking or saying.

I relate this example just to show how hard it is for us to renew our thinking about business and ministry, for-profit and non-profit, even after 30 years of being on this journey of integration.

Transforming Society requires repurposing spheres

The way to eat an elephant is one bite at a time. There are great advantages to understanding the components of a healthy society and seeking out what it means for them to be reconciled to God. Understanding these components can sharpen our focus, cause us to hone our skills, and help us to get a vision for what revival and re-formation can bring.

I have been married 30 years. I wish I had been a better student of my wife over the past three decades. I am still learning new things about her, and therefore finding better ways to serve her. One of my main tasks is to build a platform underneath her so that she can discover and walk out her full potential. My goal is not to change my wife, but to love her.

A similar principle applies to society. I can only change society if I love it. We have so misunderstood the "Do not love the world, nor the things that are in the world"[47] verse that we come to see the world as the enemy. This is in stark contrast to "God so loved the world."[48] If I understand government from God's perspective, I can love those in government. I

47 1 John 2:15
48 John 3:16

can also see the evils and pray into, work around, and confront them as needed.

I am concerned about the fact that many have become rather militant in their language about conquering mountains. I don't have to conquer what is already redeemed by God. I have to go into, love, minister to, and bring alignment to that which is already rightfully His. He knows how he wants it to look but "they" have not had anyone demonstrate what that might look like. I am an ambassador to share the constructs of a superior kingdom so that they can come into alignment with the way things were meant to be.

At The Institute—and particularly through the **rēp** Ventures— we talk about societal transformation. Our tag line is *Repurposing Business— Transforming Society®*. Our contention is that if we can see enough businesses transformed then the tide will rise in a society. Businesses aligned with God's business will create jobs, love employees, disciple them, use the business to grow them, create products that solve problems God cares about, invest in communities, etc. etc. In our early phases of engaging in a nation we simply do business. Then, having built relationships with people of peace, we draw alongside corporations to help repurpose them. We generally aim at repurposing 100 companies in order to gain critical mass. In the follow-on work we come alongside and help them steward the new purpose God has revealed for their business, growing their capacities, and ensuring that they have the wisdom to implement the revelation.

We also begin to identify the critical spheres of society and work to see specific sectors of society repurposed. None of this is a quick fix. The many parables Jesus told about the kingdom make it clear that there is a process involved in establishing the kingdom. We do not have a formula, but we do have a passion and we are growing our competencies starting with the area of Business, and spreading to the spheres that are most prominent in any particular city or nation. We see the value of understanding the spheres of influence, loving them, serving them, and aligning them with eternal truth. We generally start with Business because that is where there are the most openings. Then we move to whatever adjacent spheres are most strategic. Ultimately every sphere needs to be repurposed if society is to be transformed and the nations discipled.

I am reminded of the way things were in the beginning of time, as recorded in the book of Genesis. Here God clearly states that he had not introduced certain plants and species because there was no man "to serve the ground."[49] What a beautiful reminder that we are called to collaborate with

49   Genesis 2:5 (read in different translations)

God in bringing his order and productivity to the earth! We serve before we conquer.

We cannot do the work of repurposing spheres of society on our own. We have started working with Business, Healthcare, and Capital. We have our eye on Government and Media, and plan to follow God's leading into other sectors over time. There is a catch, however. We tend to like the comfort of our own little molehill. We burrow there, get to know the inhabitants, we settle, and we become part of the landscape. So God has to find a way to remind us that we are mountain movers, not molehill hobbits.

Dislodged by difficulty

I have a friend who is a money manager. Clients give her funds, and she invests in order to give the clients a good return. She is skilled in researching markets and choosing investment portfolios to meet the goals and risk profiles of her investors. Money management is risk management. The higher the risk, the higher the return—this is the theory. My friend made an investment in another nation. It did not go as planned and she discovered politicians had interfered and frozen the assets. This made it impossible for her to provide her clients with the returns they expected. She periodically asked for prayer.

One day we were having breakfast and it struck me what was going on. She lives on the "Capital" world and hoped to go in, make an investment, get a return, and get out. But God is less interested in the Capital molehill than he is the discipling of the nation. So he sent her a problem... courtesy of the government of that country. She is no shrinking violet, so she tackled the government, sending the president a letter saying that she would expose the corruption if he did not act. He didn't, so she dispatched news briefs to many major media outlets. Being a woman of prayer she also engaged local intercessors, sought help from the elders of the city, etc. etc. As we had breakfast it struck me: she was narrowly focused on one sector of society (Capital) and God sent her a problem that caused her to spread his aroma across many other spheres: government, religion, media, law and business. As she worked with church leaders she also learned the plight of local family, education and healthcare matters. She was dislodged by difficulty, forced from her molehill into all of society.

Remember Paul; he was doing his missionary thing. The religious establishment rejected him. He went into business and had success in spreading the kingdom ("then all of Asia heard the gospel" Acts 19:10). But he knew God would send him to Rome and an opportunity came up when he was mistreated. He therefore appealed to Caesar (the Government sphere) using a legal process (Law/Legal).

We—myself included—like to build a cabin on our molehill, settle in, and stay there. God is on the move, however, and if he has to flatten your molehill, demolish your cabin and make it so uncomfortable to stay there that you move to another one... so be it. Most of us don't like change. God's process of growing us is that he trains us in one area to give us a greater sphere of influence. We have to decide to collaborate in our own growth. Do you want to be a molehill person, or a mountain person? Not every difficulty is from the devil, so before you rebuke it or wish it away, make sure God is not expanding your territory.

Impact at the intersection of spheres

My friend's story highlights an important truth. Every sphere is important, but not every sphere is equally important in every nation. The location, history, natural resources, political and cultural factors in most nations mean that some spheres come first when it comes to transforming society. Moreover, a city or nation can maximize its impact when key spheres intersect to pursue joint strategies of transformation. There is an authority that rests on corporations that master integration. This same anointing, if you like, is needed in bringing the spheres of society together to create societal impact. "For there the Lord commanded a blessing."[50] Pulling spheres together for high purposes requires humility, persistence, creativity, flexible structures, and endurance. These things come as a competence from the Spirit.

Called Corporations

My observation of cities and nations is there are certain corporations, which may or may not be businesses, that are landmarks of a society. They shape the culture, and the language of the people surrounding the corporation is colored by the Called Corporation. Such entities may or may not be Christian or "kingdom" at all, but they exist for a purpose and have influence. I believe, of course, that if Jesus died "for the joy set before him" part of that joy must include the re-call of such corporations to their intended purpose. I am therefore intent on discovering the Called Corporations in a city, praying for them, and encouraging those who have influence to bring about, or call out, the characteristics of a Called Corporation.

When you travel to Ireland you will quickly see that Guinness is a Called Corporation. It has shaped the destiny of countless thousands guided, initially, by a godly purpose. Imagine how the work of transforming society would be enhanced if we viewed key corporations as being redeemable, reconcilable to God's intent? These organizations may not be the biggest, but they capture the heart of a city. Sometimes they are industries, such

50   Psalm 133:3 NKJV

as the movie industry in Los Angeles. The East India Company was a Called Corporation in India, and eventually believers got control of the board of directors. Instead of company policy prohibiting missionaries in the country, it became the policy to fund missionaries. In the "old days" of Silicon Valley Hewlett-Packard was a Called Corporation. Today as I look out from my study over Silicon Valley, I suspect that Google is a Called Corporation in Mountain View, Apple in Cupertino, and Cisco in San Jose.

> It is the glory of God to conceal a matter; to search out a matter is the glory of kings.[51]

Think for a moment about the city where you live: who are the Called Corporations? Are they governments, NGOs, hospitals or businesses? They are not always large companies: San Francisco, for example, is a city of small businesses with selected families owning real estate and business interests.

Do these corporations know that they are called? Many do not—just as is the case for individuals and nations. God sees the call on people and companies long

The 10-Cs: Characteristics of Called Corporations

1. **Committed** to a greater good. (The ultimate being, "to glorify God.")
2. **Cleansed**: having dealt with past, and having purity in present practices.
3. **Chiropracted**: aligned in aspects of character and competence with scripture.
4. **Culture**: a biblically grounded worldview.
5. **Community**—there is effective household understanding and experience.
6. **Centurions**: the corporation has watchmen, gap-bridgers, that are looking out for the welfare of their city.
7. **Co-creators**: the corporation develops products and services that actively meet the needs of the city, the nation and the world.
8. **Commissioning**: they send people out.
9. **Capital-positive**: they are net-positive capital creators—financial, human, spiritual, working...
10. **City-changing**: including community and nation changing, sometime world changing.

before they do. Working with God to help others see their potential is our joy and purpose: *Repurposing leaders and corporations to discover and implement personal and corporate callings, thereby transforming communities and nations.*[52]

---

51   Proverbs 25:2
52   This is the purpose statement of The Institute for Innovation, Integration & Impact, Inc.

Repurposing Business

People have a purpose: we know this by instinct and by teaching. God has set eternity in the hearts of men. We find our ultimate meaning in the context of his story, his purpose, his big idea. We also know, if we read The Bible even briefly, that nations have a purpose. God used Egypt to incubate the nation of Israel. He designed Israel to be a prototype of God's government in a nation so that other nations would see the benefits and say, "We want to worship your God!" When Israel strayed God used other nations to punish Israel. The list goes on: nations have a purpose. It stands to reason, then, that if individuals and nations have a set purpose, then households, businesses, churches, and other corporations also have a purpose that can align with God's intention.

Don't just say, "the purpose of business is to make money" because there is much, much more than that. Many Christians in business will quote the business school mantra "the purpose of business is to maximize shareholder value" in order to give themselves a free pass, an exemption from considering the claims of Christ on their career and business. Beyond that, they live by "Christian" principles in regards to their faith, but "business principles" in regards to their work.

There are three broad worldview categories, a subject I touched on earlier:

- Pantheists: they believe that god is in everything
- Atheists: they believe there is no god. This group gives rise to humanists, or in today's terms, secular humanists. Things depend on our efforts, since there is no God, and we have to simply get on with life.
- Theists believe there is one God.

You might be forgiven for thinking that Christians in business, government and other spheres are "theists" but, for the most part, you are wrong. A CEO sat in my living room recently. In our conversation I told him that most Christians in business are Christian Humanists: they are believing in Christ for salvation, but when it comes to business they believe in themselves and other human beings. "Oh my gosh," he said, "that's me!" It was refreshing to hear him admit it. So many businesspeople presume that, since they live in the West and are Christians, their business is a "kingdom business" but their businesses are no more devoted to God's business than they are to going to Mars. We therefore developed a Kingdom Business Assessment to at least crack open their minds to think about the possibilities of what it would truly look like if Jesus took over product development or the Holy Spirit ran Human Resources.

As indicated in the discussion on households, businesses are often the keyhole to societal transformation. One of the keys that opens the lock that the enemy has on society is Repurposing Business. Of course it is not the only one (as we saw in the Transformation Impact Network competencies matrix), but it is arguably one of the most ready keys. What, then, does it mean to repurpose a business?

Every business has unique assets, people, skills and experiences to accomplish something no other business in the world can accomplish. If you own or operate a corporation—a household engaged in offering services or goods—we work with you to identify where your position intersects with society's greatest needs and help you or your corporation determine how to meet them. We will ask questions to uncover your organization's unique Purpose, align your business with a higher calling, and make it a deliberate contributor to society. This involves aligning all facets of the business behind your Purpose, with supporting Foundational Principles, Strategies, Action Items and Key Performance Indicators for all drivers of corporate impact (We use a model called The 10-P Model®). It is really just a very practical take on what 2 Corinthians 5 calls the "ministry of reconciliation." Since "God was in Christ reconciling the world (cosmos) to himself" it seems to be each of our jobs to reconcile every facet of our lives to Truth. Repurposing Business makes this very tangible at the corporate level, putting legs on the vague notion of "the purpose of my business is to glorify God."

When a business or corporation has been through a Repurposing Business consultation it will have a master plan to help guide every portion of the company to change lives on a deep and meaningful level, leaving a legacy for generations to come. What are the outcomes when corporations discover their real purpose? Well, it is as if the glory of God comes to that business and the employees, and the surrounding community. We will explore The Glory of God in the next section.

In this section

How we come down the Mountain of the Lord

The results of the Mountain of the Lord

Nations transformed

The Glory of God made practical

The Glory of God in an organization

The Glory of God in an individual

Glory stories from **rēp** *Ventures*

Part 5

The Glory of God

Transforming Society

How we come down the Mountain of the Lord

I do not think God intends mountain-top experiences just so that man can have an experiential encounter with God. If we come down the mountain the same as we went up, then we are missing the trail. Moses did not come down from the mountain the same as when he went up. We will create a cognitive problem for people if we teach about taking your mountain for God and it is a formula devoid of the supernatural presence of God. We must be people presented by God in order to carry the presence of God to our sphere of influence.

> Now it shall come to pass in the latter days
> That the mountain of the Lord's house
> Shall be established on the top of the mountains,
> And shall be exalted above the hills;
> And peoples shall flow to it.
> Many nations shall come and say,
> "Come, and let us go up to the mountain of the Lord,
> To the house of the God of Jacob;
> He will teach us His ways,
> And we shall walk in His paths."
> For out of Zion the law shall go forth,
> And the word of the Lord from Jerusalem.
> He shall judge between many peoples,
> And rebuke strong nations afar off;
> They shall beat their swords into plowshares,
> And their spears into pruning hooks;
> Nation shall not lift up sword against nation,
> Neither shall they learn war anymore.
> But everyone shall sit under his vine and under his fig tree, and no one shall make them afraid;
> For the mouth of the Lord of hosts has spoken.
> For all people walk each in the name of his god,
> But we will walk in the name of the Lord our God
> Forever and ever.[53]

Reflect a little on this passage for it contains a going up, a learning that is more than academic, and a coming down. The way the law and word of God will go forth is through transformed livers of mountain-found truth. The scope will be international and results will be miraculous as whole industries shift from making tanks and bombs to sustainable agriculture. Property ownership will be established, and people will earn a good living

53   Micah 4:1-5

from their own means of production. Fear of economic ups and downs will be eliminated. We will not be depending on politicians and economists for our security. There will be a permanent change in structures, infrastructures, industries and economies... "forever and ever." You may say, "This sounds too good to be true." My friend, God is good and he is true. I want him to teach me his ways so that I can walk in his paths, so that this scale of transformation will begin through me today, whether it is perfected in my time, the millennium, or in eternity.

We must come down the mountain changed:

- Carrying the glory of God.

- Instructed in the ways of God: He will teach us his ways.

- Walking in the paths of God: We will walk in his paths.

- Understanding the heart and spirit of the laws of God: We cannot just develop tactics for molehills. We must know the heart of God regarding how he wants his world to work. The law shall go forth from Zion.

- Proclaiming the word of God: "and the word of the Lord from Jerusalem"

I have a growing appreciation for the blending of various elements in the book of Deuteronomy. In a literal 'mountain of the Lord' encounter we see at least three things working together: (1) truth (The 10 Commandments), (2) presence (evidenced in physical ways—a voice, darkness, a blaze[54]) and (3) the passionate love of God for his people.

> The Lord did not set his affection on you and choose you because you were more numerous than other peoples, for you were the fewest of all peoples. But it was because the Lord loved you and kept the oath he swore to your forefathers that he brought you out with a mighty hand and redeemed you from the land of slavery, from the power of Pharaoh king of Egypt. Know therefore that the Lord your God is God; he is the faithful God, keeping his covenant of love to a thousand generations of those who love him and keep his commands.[55]

All of this resulted in the transfer of some of God's glory onto Moses. The writings of John echo this confluence of things showing the glory of God. "The Word became flesh and made his dwelling among us. We have

54 Deuteronomy 5: 23-24 When you heard the voice out of the darkness, while the mountain was ablaze with fire, all the leading men of your tribes and your elders came to me. And you said, "The Lord our God has shown us his glory and his majesty, and we have heard his voice from the fire. Today we have seen that a man can live even if God speaks with him."

55 Deuteronomy 7:7-9

seen his glory, the glory of the One and Only, who came from the Father, full of grace and truth."[56] But that was not enough to reveal the glory of God: grace is good, love is wonderful, and truth is tremendous. In the next chapter we see the rest of the story.

> This, the first of his miraculous signs, Jesus performed in Cana of Galilee. He thus revealed his glory, and his disciples put their faith in him.[57]

Later Jesus adds a fourth and fifth leg to the glory stool: his works, and the testimony of the Father. It is not enough for us to have truth without power, the testimony of man without the affirmation by God, and good intentions without good works. When we come down from the mountain we know, we shine, and we work. What sorts of things can we actually do that will make a difference at a societal level? Nehemiah gives us some models that we should re-explore with fresh eyes.

The results of the Mountain of the Lord

What are the results of us, by faith, moving the mountain of the Lord so that its affects are felt across all of society? Is it good enough to have a Christian mayor or chief of police? Is it enough that crime goes down or jobs are created?

The results of us understanding, experiencing and living from the mountain of the Lord are generally the same signs we would expect from the completion of Christ's mission: the poor hear good news, the captives are set free, the blind receive sight, etc. We tend to focus on the individual or micro-indicators and ignore the broad, societal indicators. It is easier to do this of course, and it requires a stretch to examine the indicators that describe whole cities and nations. But this need for more renewed thinking and greater faith should not short circuit our pressing through.

Churches have the same problem envisioning a transformed future. I recently asked a church leadership team, "What will your city look like five years from now if the kingdom of God comes to the city?" Most of the answers revolved around more people coming to the church. It took some prodding for them to think about infrastructure, the environment, job creation, decreased prostitution, corruption disappearing, and more.

A member of parliament (politician) told me, "Brett, there are Christians in every political party in this country, but you will never get them to agree." I replied, "I can get them to agree." He asked how and I said, "We will take them to another nation to teach them God's ways of godly government.

56   John 1:14
57   John 2:11

As they prepare to go they will need to submit their political agendas to the Word of God." This model already works for businesspeople. One result of us encountering God on his "mountain" is that we come down with his agenda, not ours. Moses was the most humble man who ever lived. Our encounters with God will not make us proud if we truly encounter Him.

God has a set of principles for operating in every sphere. I encourage us to have gatherings by sector to ask the good questions about the ways of God in that sphere. "He will teach us of his ways." We need to seek them out so that "we will walk in his paths." His laws will get written on our hearts so that we can live the kingdom with both understanding and integrity. There are many "key performance indicators" of societal transformation in scripture, and we need to look to these also in order to understand what transformation could be like in each of the spheres.

Nations transformed

Loren Cunningham shares amazing stories about national transformation. His account of the role of the Word of God, among other factors, is inspiring. One nation has gone from persecuting believers to sending tens of thousands of missionaries to the nations. This nation has gone from poverty to prosperity primarily because of massive revival.[58] Chile developed a middle class coming out of a revival in the early part of the 20th Century. Switzerland was transformed by the integrated teaching of Calvin. Today many instances of city and national transformation are being examined and documented. George Otis, Jr. and his team at Sentinel Group have done a diligent job tracking, verifying and recording these stories.[59]

The Glory of God made practical

Jesus, more than anyone else who has been on this planet, made the glory of God tangible. Those reading this book know that our purpose is to "glorify God." The problem is that this is a phrase that is hard to unpack. The answer, again, is found in the life of Jesus. If we can look at how he revealed glory, then we can get a leg-up in thinking more clearly about what it might look like to see the glory of God come to each sphere of society.

We have already considered various "legs" to the throne where God's glory is evident; there are no doubt many more windows into the glory of God, but to keep things simple I have limited the view to four:

- Grace
- Truth

---

58   **The Book that Transforms Nations**, Loren Cunningham, YWAM Singapore Publishing

59   See www.glowtorch.org for examples. While no reporting is flawless, we have verified the journalistic standards of Sentinel and find them to exceed those of mainstream media.

- Miracles (signs and wonders)
- Works.

Now let's apply this framework to each sphere of society. The goal is not to be definitive because, as Moses and team found out, God can reveal his glory however he wants to do it. The purpose of thinking this through is to make our own minds more malleable to the purposes of God for each sphere. First, let's start with Business since this is an area where we have worked with hundreds of companies trying to get definition on this matter.

SPHERE	ELEMENTS OF GLORY	A FEW SAMPLE KINGDOM INDICATORS
BUSINESS	Grace	Businesses operate with an ease, a grace-enablement from God to do business as ministry to God, and to reveal the compassion and nature of the Father through their work.
	Truth	• Ethics are exemplary, no corruption, and no excuse for exploitation under the banner of "this is business." • Business people are seeking out the ways of God in regards to business and are operating from a higher set of principles—Foundational Principles—that are better than 'best practices.'
	Miracles	• Continual revelation of new products, and wineskins/operating models. • The unabashed embracing and celebration of God's miraculous interventions in the daily life of business.
	Works	• Businesses are bent on doing things that have an eternal impact. • Plans, budgets, products and operations—all facets of business—are geared towards eternity while simultaneously expecting, experiencing and rejoicing in rewards on earth. Why? Because God is good, and he is "the rewarder of those who diligently seek him."

Sticking with the order used previously we will move to Capital, a sphere whose rampant excesses have crippled many economies. Capital has not, it seems, been transformed—there is no evidence of the repurposing of capital at the time of this writing. Rather than curse the darkness, however, we should contemplate what capital markets would look like if they radiated the glory of God.

SPHERE	ELEMENTS OF GLORY	A FEW SAMPLE KINGDOM INDICATORS
CAPITAL	Grace	Capital is being used to enable godly initiatives, blessing society while building wealth for many, not just a few.
	Truth	• Kingdom capitalists are using capital with clear intentions, pure motives, and the desire to fund initiatives that offer a good return for risk while intentionally furthering the greater good of society. • There is a shift away from control-oriented, passive income that enslaves the debtor/borrower. • We have a new practice of storehouse, where funds are gathered for God's projects.
	Miracles	• Excellent returns on breakthrough innovations, many of which have been revealed supernaturally, and proven diligently. • We are routinely open to many sources of capital. • We grow and flow capital freely.
	Works	• There is a routine building—as opposed to redistribution—of wealth as those gifted in this area enable everyday people to become wealth creators. • People are shifting away from hand-outs to hand-ups.

Moving to Government: we all agree that "righteousness exalts a nation"[60] and good government creates a peaceful, just environment where citizens are able to worship freely, work meaningfully, provide for their own needs, and serve a common national purpose. Simply put, we want the favor of God on our nations. The truth is that favor comes from an increase of God's government. This has nothing to do with the 'God the Republican' or "God the Independent /Democratic / whatever" philosophy that pervades some initiatives aimed at societal reform. Isaiah says, "Of the increase of his government and peace there shall be no end."[61] To get the peace of God we need the government of God. This starts with self-governance submitted to Christ. Call it surrender, yielding to the lordship of Christ, if you like. Political maneuvering is meaningless if we are not yielded in this primary manner.

60   Proverbs 13:34
61   Isaiah 9:7

The Glory of God   121

Building on this a little, we live at a time in history where there is an opportunity for an increase of the governance of God. Why? In short, things are not working very well. Finances are in the tank and, this is causing an increase in personal disciplines, less frivolous spending, and more thoughts about saving and better investing. The medicine may not be nice, but the outcome could be good. A positive outcome from the global economic meltdown is not an automatic, however, because we as people may not turn to God. Let's remember the progression:

1. We cast off restraint, fiscally at least.

2. The economic models on which we relied were found wanting.

3. We stood at a crossroads and faced two choices:
   a. Rely more on God while reevaluating our financial patterns.
   b. Rely more on government while spending our way out of trouble.

This is not a political analysis, but a spiritual audit of our response to crisis. The US as a nation has turned to government, not God, at this point. More government spending, government bailouts, cash-for-clunker car purchase assistance, extended unemployment, and the gargantuan health care approach. We have to ask ourselves, "If we as the Church were remembering the poor, caring for the environment, praying for elected representatives and those in office, delaying gratification and running businesses with equity, would we need so much government?"

A second factor is how technology is putting legs on democracy. Free information and communication leads to thoughts, no surprise, of freedom. So whole nations are, at the time of writing, questioning the undemocratic reign of their leaders. Access to information is translating to a demand for leaders to be more accessible and transparent. A reality of today's world is that there are fewer places for bad leaders to hide.

Psalm 72 is the prayer of a father, David, for his son, Solomon, and has a focus on how the wise son would govern. It is filled with phrases like justice, righteousness, judging fairly, defending the afflicted, delivering the needy, taking pity on the weak, and saving the needy from death.

Micah is simply eloquent in his summary of three characteristics of a nation that is reflecting God's government.

> He has showed you, O man, what is good. And what does the Lord require of you? To act justly and to love mercy and to walk humbly with your God [62]

---

[62]   Micah 6:8

SPHERE	ELEMENTS OF GLORY	A FEW SAMPLE KINGDOM INDICATORS
GOVERNMENT	Grace	• Leaders operating in the fear of God, demonstrating wisdom, cognizant of the fact that they are accountable to God and will give an account to him. • Fathers and mothers leading nations. • The taxes collected and services offered will be equitable for the situation.
	Truth	• Transparent reporting, servant leadership, entrusting others with life decisions, empowering them to be better citizens, clear accountability, timely communications. • Decision making that is based on eternal principles, not short term gains. • There may well be separation of church and state, but there will not be a separation of God and government.
	Miracles	• The nation will produce more than is logical, it will lend to other nations, but borrow from none. • There will be high levels of productivity with measures that capture the truth of outputs, not just GDP. • God will cause opposition to come from one direction but flee in seven.
	Works	• Corruption free, selfless, servant-oriented, practical programs of mercy, compassion and love for citizenry. • Infrastructure will be built, maintained and stewarded as a trust. • A peaceful environment will be created in which people can fulfill their God-given potential.

When it comes to Law the book of Isaiah 28 points out an interesting paradox: when people reject God they get more rules. The world tells us, "Do not follow God because he will kill your joy with his rules." That is a defamation of God's character. Verses 5 and 6 of Isaiah 28 say,

> In that day the Lord Almighty will be a glorious crown, a beautiful wreath for the remnant of his people. He will be a spirit of justice to him who sits in judgment, a source of strength to those who turn back the battle at the gate.

God himself offers to infuse the legal system with his own spirit, "a spirit of justice." But man would have none of it, and they ended up needing more laws to compensate for the lack of the Spirit's influence. Verses 10-13 go on to say:

> "For it is: Do and do, do and do, rule on rule, rule on rule; a little here, a little there." Very well then, with foreign lips and strange tongues God will speak to this people, to whom he said, "This is the resting place, let the weary rest"; and, "This is the place of repose"—but they would not listen. So then, the word of the Lord to them will become: Do and do, do and do, rule on rule, rule on rule; a little here, a little there—so that they will go and fall backward, be injured and snared and captured.

As we come to consider what the glory of God looks like in the Legal sector, let's be careful to not slip back into legalism, but reach for the law of the Spirit written on the hearts of mankind. I did a Google search on "lawlessness" within the News category and it returned over 1,400 articles for just one week. The Legal sphere needs reformation—what would it look like for this sphere to be marked by the glory of God?

SPHERE	ELEMENTS OF GLORY	A FEW SAMPLE KINGDOM INDICATORS
LAW	Grace	• Gentle justice, strength for the needy. • Laws that do not respect persons. • Redemptive and restorative justice.
	Truth	• Principled law giving, alignment of laws with God's revealed truth. • Clearly articulated and documented law. • Principled application of the law. • Zero corruption.
	Miracles	• Criminal activity decreased. • Prisons emptying. • Revival across judicial systems, including law enforcement, such as we are seeing in parts of Brazil, etc. • Conspiracies uncovered.
	Works	• Legal aid for needy, representation for those without means. • Restitution where legal action deprived people of what was theirs. • Decrease in frivolous lawsuits. • Consistent rule of law, appropriate access to legal resources for all. • Decrease of loopholes, fewer people taking advantage of others, closing of illegal gaps created by the law.

In the Old Testament things were more integrated than they are today. Social work, if you like, was integrated into the fabric of life. Businesses were meant to be generous, leaving a portion for the poor. Everyone was supposed to be kind to foreigners. Special gifts were to be given to those in need on a routine basis: one example was that one's tithe, every third year, was to be given to the poor. Social security was everyone's job. Today we have groups focused on human rights, slavery, education, clean water, land mine removal and many other noble causes. The operating model, as a reminder, is often donation driven. These non-governmental organizations (NGOs) meet genuine needs, but they can also develop an agenda that is based off a philosophy that is not biblical. Take, for example, the groups that advocate population control: their assumptions and methods can be counter to Judeo-Christian ethics.

Yet, as with all sectors, NGOs can reflect the glory of God. What might this look like?

SPHERE	ELEMENTS OF GLORY	A FEW SAMPLE KINGDOM INDICATORS
NGO	Grace	<ul><li>Loving people more than loving one's cause.</li><li>Caring for everyone because they are made in God's image, not because it makes us look successful.</li><li>Doing good because it's the right thing to do, not because it makes us feel good.</li></ul>
	Truth	<ul><li>Basing the work on clear principles, openly stated.</li><li>No masked or hidden agendas..</li></ul>
	Miracles	<ul><li>Good that happens beyond the natural resources available: food is multiplied, medicines don't run out, rain comes, etc.</li><li>Deeper needs are addressed at the same time as obvious needs.</li></ul>
	Works	<ul><li>Doing the work to serve, and not to get publicity, more funds, or greater influence.</li><li>Elevating beneficiaries from recipients to participants.</li><li>Those who receive aid go on to give aid.</li></ul>

Family comes under a lot of pressure precisely because God has a family, and our families are supposed to reveal his family.

God sets the lonely in families.[63]

This is still his plan. The Church, at the macro level, is the family of God and he is the Father.

63   Psalm 68:6

SPHERE	ELEMENTS OF GLORY	A FEW SAMPLE KINGDOM INDICATORS
FAMILY	Grace	• People live in families with unconditional love. • The brokenness of humankind is healed in environments of love. • The generations love each other—"turn the hearts of the fathers to their children, and the hearts of the children to their fathers." (Malachi 4:6) • We exhibit grace to extend household beyond those who look like us.
	Truth	• Fathers and mothers accurately reflect the nature of God, as best human beings can. • A right understanding of fathers, mothers and children. • Clear constructs of inter-generational stewardship and passing on of spiritual heritage.
	Miracles	• Families will have children. • Singles will find godly spouses. • Sons will find fathers they never had, and the childless will have many children. • Families will once again reflect the attributes of God.
	Works	• Lonely will be welcomed, set in families. • We will routinely practice hospitality... every day. • The giant of isolation will be torn down by the practical kindness of those reaching beyond their comfort zones. • Community will be rediscovered. • We will shift from being an I-me-orphan people to an us-we-family people.

At the micro level, biological families are representative of God. Then there are spiritual families where spiritual fathers organically lead many. Broken homes, children who never know their fathers and "act out" in society, fathers who are unclear as to their role in the home and society... these all diminish our ability to imagine God's glory in the sphere of family. We create organizations to fix the problems when we should be fixing families. Can we renew Family if we do not rightly connect to God as Father? What would it look like if we really knew, experienced and walked in the fatherhood of God?

The Glory of God 127

God is in Media. We cannot deny that he is the best communicator in the universe with a diverse, integrated media campaign that should be the envy of Madison Avenue. Nature, the spoken word, the written word, signs and wonders—he speaks in many ways. A core tenet of the Christian faith is that God is, and he is not silent.

We accept that he speaks to us personally; it is harder for us to imagine him speaking through Media. I know that there are separate TV channels, radio stations and magazines. Would it not be wonderful to encounter unvarnished truth through Media? I am not asking to imagine separate, however, but integrated. It is one thing to have GOD-TV and perhaps another to have God on everyday TV getting his message across in the public square. And it's more than the message, but the assumptions, agenda and mode of communication too.

There is a word of caution, however: I recently read an article decrying the failures of the Boomer generation in Media and the burgeoning success of the newer generations. My comment (in a blogpost, of course) to the author was that you don't make good wine out of sour grapes. We need a generation that stands for something positive, and not simply against the previous generation. (The Boomers already did that.)

> *"All of us who professionally use the mass media are the shapers of society. We can vulgarize that society. We can brutalize it. Or we can help lift it onto a higher level."*
>
> *William Bernbach*
> *(American advertising executive, 1911-1982)*

SPHERE	ELEMENTS OF GLORY	A FEW SAMPLE KINGDOM INDICATORS
MEDIA	Grace	• It would reflect redemption and hope. • The viewer/participant* would realize they can make a difference. (*Note: With the advent of social media we are moving away from passive viewership and toward a reemergence of participation and activism). • Tough issues would be depicted compassionately, with an eye on redemption.
	Truth	• Media is conveying truth routinely. Good news is the dominant news, and light is broadcast more than darkness. Truth is exalted, not twisted, and people are intrigued with what is right, not what is perverted. • It would inspire empathy and reveal a commonality between people, and their need for redemption. It would show characters and situations that were fallen and not perfect (thus revealing the truth of the human condition). • Characters would have the opportunity to pursue or not pursue holiness through free will. • Media would point to Christ by elevating that which is true, good and beautiful.
	Miracles	• Redemptive stories miraculously find their way into the news, effectively carrying the testimonies of Jesus. • People are set free, encouraged, loved and healed through these testimonies. • Miracles would be more commonplace. Faith in the unseen would frequently be a precursor to miracles.
	Works	• Truth is uncovered, sought out, packaged and presented. All forms of media come alive with the dynamic of God, the Word. • Truth of the fallen human condition is uncovered and presented with opportunity for redemption through his grace. • Media would represent the highest quality of excellence as all forms of media become a high priesthood celebrating the goodness of God and making Christ known.

There is a distinction between serving God and playing god. This is a danger in any of the spheres, and when Healthcare becomes its own god then it can lead to Determinism... determining, at worst, who lives and dies, and at least, who is entitled to healthcare. Many, many healthcare professionals work because they are called to be part of God's healing army. We still have a long way to go, however, before the kingdom of God is fully evident in this crucial sector of society, and opportunities for a greater measure of God's glory abound.

SPHERE	ELEMENTS OF GLORY	A FEW SAMPLE KINGDOM INDICATORS
HEALTHCARE	Grace	<ul><li>Healthcare is delivered with compassion, regardless of the social condition of the recipient.</li><li>Healthcare providers work as a calling, not just a profession.</li></ul>
	Truth	The assumptions of the healthcare providers are based on the fact that God is our creator, he fashioned us, and we are built by design.
	Miracles	<ul><li>Healthcare providers pray with patients, blending medical science and spirituality in an integrated manner, without one supplanting the other.</li><li>Healing is commonplace.</li></ul>
	Works	<ul><li>New cures are becoming evident for long standing illnesses. There is breakthrough based on revelation and research.</li><li>Healthcare funding is based on true compassion, not false ideology.</li></ul>

The act of educating generally builds positive assets in a society. Teachers and educators are often dedicated people called to their profession. What one has to consider is the philosophy of education that is prevalent in a city, state or nation. The philosophy of education can be described as the "application of philosophical methods to the theory and practice of education. Among the topics investigated in the philosophy of education are the nature of learning, especially in children; the purpose of education, particularly the question of whether the chief goal of educators should be imparting knowledge, developing intellectual independence, or instilling moral or political values; the nature of education-related concepts, including the concept of education itself; the sources and legitimacy of educational authority; and the conduct of educational research."

As worldview shifts the assumptions about "the sources of legitimacy of educational authority" come into question. Every sphere has its dangers, but in Education we can start with a genuine desire to grow in learning and end up making an idol of our minds

SPHERE	ELEMENTS OF GLORY	A FEW SAMPLE KINGDOM INDICATORS
EDUCATION	Grace	• Every person is valued and given an opportunity to be educated, regardless of their social status, gender or ability to afford such education. • Educators look for and develop the potential of those being educated. • The education goes beyond the accumulation of knowledge and information, but involves "the spirit of wisdom and revelation."
	Truth	• There is clarity about what truth is absolute, and what is relative, what is known, and what is speculation. • There is a celebration of "that which is pure, noble, trustworthy, of good report." • Truth is spiritually discerned as well as intellectually grasped. • We follow Jesus' model of Identity, then Action, then Understanding (rather than Learning, Understanding, Action)
	Miracles	• The abilities of people are lifted through a combination of hard work, inspiration, and the inspired development of new faculties. • Breakthroughs in learning come in response to a deep desire to know God more, and to seek him first.
	Works	• Education becomes the collective work of many organizations, including family and business. It is not left to those with a vocation in Education alone. • Integrated learning produces .

I have already pointed out why I don't think that "church" and "missions" are spheres of society. Religion is a sphere, however, and every society worships something, or many things. What does it look like when society sees and acknowledges the one true God as being on his throne? We quickly trivialize God, but a quick read of the book of Revelation and his might, awe and unstoppable purposes will quickly re-infuse a healthy respect for Him. The Church needs repurposing. Too often it serves the agenda of man or uses the mechanisms of man, and drifts from its anchor.

What would it look like if Religion was repurposed? How would it be if the glory of God permeated the dry place of religion and made it alive and real with something beyond the mere concoctions of man?

SPHERE	ELEMENTS OF GLORY	A FEW SAMPLE KINGDOM INDICATORS
RELIGION	Grace	• The graciousness of God is evident and permeates society. • The Church lifts burdens; it does not place legalistic burdens on people • Churches are not perceived to be judgemental and divisive, but accepting and caring. • Spiritual parents give wings to the next generation, who remain loyal to them.
	Truth	• Truth is upheld without apology, and without bigotry. • Integrity surpasses politics. • Hypocrisy is nowhere to be seen: there is no disconnect between our standards for others and our walk with God. • Unity is celebrated, division a thing of the past.
	Miracles	• People see miracles routinely. • Skepticism melts in light of the presence of God and related miracles. • The Word of God is confirmed by the Power of God.
	Works	• Churches do good things for society, routinely serving as instruments of God's compassion, and his creativity in developing solutions to real needs. • Fruit is more abundant than theory; completed works overshadow excuses for not working with God. • The Church is a net contributor to society.

In the book of Revelation letters are written to the city-church in seven cities. In every instance the answer to their problem is Jesus—how he introduces himself is, in fact, the remedy to their problem. The same is true in the spheres of society: Jesus is the answer.

We become what we focus on. Our horizon should be filled with Jesus, not giants, strongmen or ruined foundations. Actively use your mind to imagine what it will look like when he is:

- CEO
- Judge/Advocate, Chief Justice

- Financier, Minister of Economics
- Provost, Dean
- Chief Physician, Minister of Health
- Patriarch
- President, Prime Minister
- Media mogul
- Chairman
- Father.... Lord

The prophet Isaiah put it this way:

> Of the increase of his government and peace there shall be no end.[64]

The Glory of God in an organization

We have talked a fair amount about what it looks like for the glory of God to come to a particular sphere of society. The reality is that society is made up of lots of households, and households have ways in which they function. The core of this functioning can be described as the Operating Model of the corporation. For those from a Religious, or Christian, background you may understand the term "wineskin" more than "operating model." Any number of factors can help an organization increase its impact. At The Institute we have identified ten drivers of organizational impact, and we call this The 10-P Model. You can think of these as ten spokes in the back wheel of a bicycle, and the front wheel (representing Character) also has ten drivers of personal impact, The 10-Fs. A more comprehensive coverage of this model is contained in **I-Operations**.[65]

We help corporations determine ways in which they can implement biblical principles in each of the 10 areas. Assuming this has been done, what might it look like to glorify God—giving him honor, credit, worth—through each of these ten areas? Likewise, how can the ten drivers of personal impact specifically give glory to God.

---

64 Isaiah 9:7
65 I-Operations: How the Internet can transform your Operating Model, Daichendt and Johnson, Indaba Publishing

Purpose

The organization has the same purpose as God. Whatever it does is as a subsidiary of God, Inc. It represents truth, or communicates truth. It is real to the core, and has a timeless quality. There is consistency between the purpose and the work, or business, of the organization. The business or organization spreads peace, favor and grace to all of its stakeholders, not allowing the quest for efficiency to override the "soft side" of the love of God.

Product

There is supernatural input into product design; new products reflect the order, creativity, joy, care and intervention of God. The product development is itself characterized by creativity, inspiration, new inventions, and ideas to tackle problems that are on the heart of God. The products provide breakthrough solutions that leave people saying, "This can only have been God." Companies are laying hands on their products and praying that the end customers will be touched for good when they experience the products.

Positioning

The corporation's positioning reflects how God sees the organization and the role he has for it to play in His context. The corporation is at peace with who it is, believing God for great things while simultaneously working within the mandate God has given. This right positioning results in the organization being blessed, and having authority to extend the kingdom of God. It then functions from a place of settled identity that is counter to the usual self-promotion and posturing.

Presence

Organizations are using the reach of their products to extend the reach of God's goodness towards society. Businesses, schoolhouses and libraries are hosting the presence of God. The ethos of the company is resulting in spiritual capital that takes the goods and services far beyond the reach of traditional marketing. The power of ordinary people sharing good news—becoming product and business evangelists—extends the influence of even small businesses into the farthest corners of the earth. Where products go, the presence of God goes with them.

Partnering

Christians are practicing redemptive partnering, using business and other collaboration as a way to disciple partners. Principles of reconciliation, love and caring are being infused into business contracts, and trust is being built. As people learn to trust God's people a foundation is laid for them to trust the people's God. The unity evident between the Father, Son and Spirit is flowing over into relationships between marketplace ministers. Jesus is seeing the answer to his John 17 prayer, "that they may be one." The world is marveling as they see how we love each other, and not just in the prayer meeting; we love each other's businesses too. We promote each other's churches, support each other's art shows, and give money to our "competition" when God tells us to do so. We send our best employee to another corporation so that he or she can disciple them.

Process

The processes value integrity over profit, and acknowledge that there is a right way to do things. The end does not always justify the means. Prayer is incorporated into core business and other processes, thereby demonstrating reliance on God. There is a habit of "inquiring of the Lord." Processes are fair, affirming the value of all stakeholders, including employees. Intercession is a core competence, and everyone understands the biblical basis for work.

People

The organizations, especially businesses that have people on site for most of their awake time, are committed to instilling "truth in the inner being" of people. Internal alignment, integration of all facets of life, and non-dichotomized living become the norm. The corporation identifies and removes the walls between Career, Calling, Community and Creativity, which is part of its task in tearing down strongholds. People therefore are free to discover and walk out their calling in the context of their work, and they do their work as worship.

They require the minimum of management supervision because they are working for God, not just their employer, and they do their work for God first, and man second. Genuine community exists in the workplace, and people love each other. Colleagues give to each other, bless each other, and spur each other on to new levels of leadership. Prayer is routine and integral to work, not a separate activity.

Planning

Planning begins with asking God his plans. Remembering what he has done, planning takes place in an atmosphere of faith. God's goals trump the organization's goals, and the company learns to surrender and collaborate with God. The company has wise counselors, but does not substitute dependence on man in place of dependence on God. Plans include a faith stretch and God is invited to bridge the gap. Plans are continually evaluated, and held fluidly before God. There is the good combination of faith and order.

Place

The splendor of God's nature is seen in the physical place, and the sense of who God is can be felt in the spirit. There is calm, beauty and order in the facilities, and yet employees or associates have made their space personal to them. The purpose of the organization is reflected in the space, hospitality creates a welcome, and the values of the corporation are reinforced through the physical space. Where needed, past wrongs have been rectified—the land has been restored, spiritually speaking—and restitution has been made if the land was acquired in a wrong manner. Visitors to the organization experience the presence of God in surprising and often un-orchestrated ways.

Profit

The right measures of success are in place: assets are grown, wealth is created, and flow-through is at a miraculous level. There is a complete freedom from greed, and Mammon has no foothold in the corporation. The financing is marked by favor, and the uncommon obedience of the corporation creates a draw of customers, employees and other stakeholders to the corporation. The activity of "locusts" is minimal, and the corporation is blessed to be a blessing. Those who bring value to the company are honored in ways that include the giving of first fruits. The corporation blesses the poor through job creation, generosity and hand-ups.

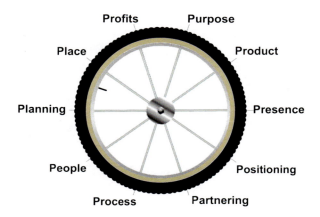

The Glory of God in an individual

The drivers of personal impact also reflect the glory of God. We have elaborated on the basic ideas of the facets of our lives that have to be healthy in order for us to have a positive personal impact.

Family

Biological families and spiritual families are committed to reflecting the attributes of the Father. They know that they take their identity from him, and they live according to his design in order to honor him. The purpose of the family is not the family, but the Father.

Work is family too, and people work in a household, not an orphanage. Love is pure, being both tough and gracious as the situation requires. Fathers and mothers in the corporation are honored, and those younger in the faith are celebrated, given opportunities to grow, and released as they mature. Leaders seldom "pull rank" and are committed to serving others. There is a genuine enjoyment in being together. There is a real desire for individuals and the household to grow, and people do not coast, or slack off, just because they are part of the family.

Fun

We are remembering to be like little children, and we are spending time playing with God, not just working for God. Many people have discovered the connection between the joy of the Lord and fun; they are in the same bucket. We laugh at ourselves, laugh with others, and give delight to our Dad. We know when to rest and when to work. We remember not to take ourselves too seriously.

Fitness

We neither neglect nor worship our own bodies. We have appropriate fitness, and good eating habits. Healing is the norm, and as the people of God we are gaining victory over all forms of illness. We look to God, not government, as the securer of our health. There is a sense of wellbeing that emanates from us in response to walking in the glory of God.

Feelings

We are filled with joy, going beyond emotional stability to exuding a deep joy in God. We are convinced that he is pleased with us, and enjoys us. We behave in ways that are governed more by Christ than culture, by the Spirit than circumstances. We have overcome the curses of isolation, fear of man, introspection and bitterness. We are a forgiven and forgiving people

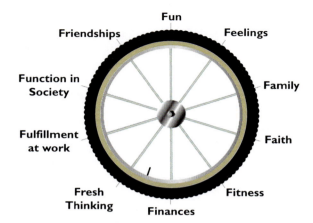

who have a generosity of spirit and a breadth and depth of heart. We don't blame the past or others for who we are. We have joy in today, and are hopeful of a bright future.

Faith

We are discovering fresh vistas of faith daily, not content to live within the limits of yesterday's victories. We are moving from glory to glory, from victory to victory. Even as circumstances get less favorable, we are a people of unswerving trust in the fact that God is good. We realize that the type of filter through which we sift what comes our way is essential, and we are keeping it clean: therefore we assume that God is good, and the things that assail us he intends for good. We are a people who are expecting to do mighty exploits, believing that what we have seen to date is nothing compared to what God will still accomplish through us.

Friendships

We reflect the unity and special relationship within the Godhead by being in relationship with fellow followers. We have naturally supernatural relationships, enjoying, serving and honoring each other. We feel good around our friends, yet keep the circle open for new brothers and sisters who constantly join our community. We are friends with Jesus, and we understand his business.

Fulfillment at Work

We love work because we love the God who made work, and who himself works to this day. We are not slack, we are not lazy, and we are not afraid of laboring. We know, however, that our work is worship, and we are desperate to co-labor with God in the work he is doing. We know that the work we do on earth is preparation, a skills building phase, for the work we might well be doing for eternity. We accept responsibility because it means that the kingdom is being furthered through our redeemed work.

Function in Society

We are living in the truth that God has given us a specific role to play in society, following the example of Jesus in bringing hope, life, healing and deliverance to all. We are standing on tiptoes to see how we can be a part of seeing the full implications of the influence of Jesus coming to our neighborhoods and cities. We are intervening lovingly and creatively in the challenges (giants) of society. We are being an example of the character and works of God, rather than speaking to society about what they should be doing. We love the society enough to be in it, and to transform it.

Fresh Thinking

We are humble enough to know that only a fraction of the things in the infinite mind of Christ has been seen by man. We do not even know the ends of the universe, let alone what God wants to still do on earth with man. We are therefore inquiring of God, seeking him with our whole beings, asking him about the things that are on his heart. This inquisitiveness comes from intimacy, not arrogance, from nearness not intellectualism. Our ideas are springing from clear spirits, rested minds and pure hearts. We are learning to ask the right questions, and the answers God is giving are putting people of faith in positions of influence, although they are not grabbing for them. Rigorous research and simple inspiration are both valued; inspiration is followed by faithful implementation.

Finances

We have come to understand God's economy and how it differs from "the world system." We have, through understanding and generosity, been schooled in financial freedom. We know without doubt that God is our source, and we seek him for varied streams of income, not to become independent of him, but to boast in his good provision. We manage expenses, delaying gratification until we can truly afford things, and seeking to save, invest and bless. We are not afraid of creating wealth and see this as the mark of God's people. We know that the purpose of money is to give Jesus the return to which he is entitled, to help us fulfill our purposes in him, to provide for our needs, to bless others, to complete the work of God, and to provide a platform of multi-faceted capital for future generations.

Jacob knew that the thing that fills our vision as we work is what we will reproduce. In his case he received a divine strategy for breeding strong, speckled sheep. In Genesis 30 we read how he placed the striped poplar branches in front of the strong sheep while they drank and mated, and they produced strong, speckled sheep. We need a stronger vision of the glory of God in front of us as we work so that we will produce what is in our vision.

Glory stories from **rēp** Ventures

The very phrase, "glory story", sounds tacky and you can imagine the gaudy Christian sub-culture that comes with it. The reality of God's glory is anything but religious or tacky. Since God uses signs and wonders as part of his marketing, we routinely pray for miracles in business. We then document these miracles on Marketplace Miracle forms and have the clients sign-off to indicate that the miracle is legitimate. (We don't want the stories to grow or shrink with the re-telling.)

When it comes to societal transformation the combination of grace, truth, power and works can be different for each sphere. Here is a small slice of "God showing up" in the business world we have seen:

- Broken equipment fixed by prayer: Cranes, mother boards, car wash, etc.
- Computers, overhead projectors and other gadgets fixed
- Defects in production lines go from 25% to 0% in one day after prayer
- Miraculous orders for clothing inventory that was 18 months out of fashion
- Sales cycles dropped from 9 months to 45 days with no change in sales practices
- Debts recovered, and debts settled
- Property sold, bought, given and received
- Government contracts granted
- National Wireless and TV licences granted to companies with only two employees.
- Law suits settled after God woke both parties at the same time on the same night and convicted them
- Businesses sold (as in, "What would it take for God to show you that he cared about your business" my friend Kim asked a businessman in Cape Town. "I want to sell a branch operation." The next day a buyer called and bought the branch. The businessman was turned

around. A few years later the purchaser called and said that sales at the branch he acquired were not going well. "Just pray and ask God to give you sales," said our client. They prayed and the next day sales were the best ever. Miracles beget miracles.)

- Many brand new product ideas given in dreams and visions and inspirations

These are in addition to the more "normal" miracles such as:

- Food multiplied
- Food, and other, allergies healed
- Marriages healed, reconciled
- Inter-generational healing
- Childless couples conceiving
- People coming to know God through Jesus Christ.

What do we do with this increased and direct engagement of God in so many new and deliberate ways? How do businesspeople, teachers and politicians respond to God invading their tidy space? We can get caught up in the miracles themselves, which is not a good thing. We can ignore them, forgetting that those who have seen or experienced miracles have a greater responsibility. Or we can rightly see them as God's underscoring of the importance of our work and his desire to engage with us.

We can imagine the glory of God; we must also be attuned to His timing. Since God is interested in nations, it is important to understand his ways when it comes to the seasons or phases of nationhood.

The Glory of God 141

In this section

Phases of development

The cycle can be broken

Where does the Church fit into this?

Micro-ordering can have unintended outcomes

Part 6

Phases of Nationhood

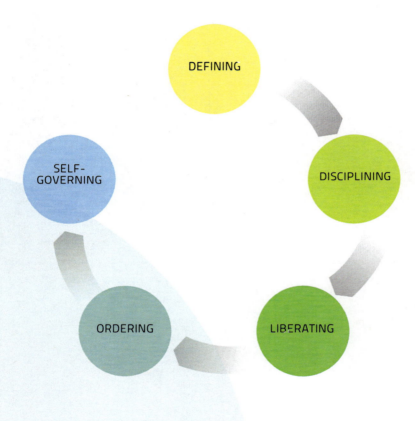

Figure 8: There are five phases which precede a nation's progression to transformation. Understanding where any nation fits in this cycle is essential to effective societal transformation.

Phases of development

The Church has a critical role to play in the discipling of a nation. It is not a guaranteed role, however, and we are arrogant if we do not recognize how the very success we seek in impacting society can carry the seeds of self-aggrandizement and failure. History shows this is true for politicians, generals and business leaders: the temptation to get one's fingers in the proverbial till is as true for religious leaders as it is for communist bureaucrats.

Jesus assured us, as we focus on preaching the kingdom, he will build his Church. The first few centuries after Christ reveal a vibrant church positively impacting the lives of everyday people. There were 50,000 widows and orphans served by the church in Constantinople alone. In time, the servers became the served, and a calling to minister became a career in ministry. The poor remained poor, and the church became rich.

While this is a gross simplification of a few centuries of church history, we should agree that we often focus on building the church and ignore the kingdom of God. We get the reverse of what we hoped for: researchers are not short of indicators that church-as-we-know-it is under threat. Membership in traditional denominations has declined in many countries. Church attendance is dismally low in some Western nations. Emerging generations are questioning the validity of the building-based institutional church. You could argue, based on some data, the church is losing its relevance in modern society.

> A large and growing number of Americans who avoid congregational contact are not rejecting Christianity as much as they are shifting how they interact with God and people in a strategic effort to have a more fulfilling spiritual life. This suggests that we are on the precipice of a new era of spiritual experience and expression.[66]

Nonetheless, Jesus is doing his job, the Church is being built, and the numerical growth of his people on the planet is exponential. Estimates are that 30,000 believers are baptized in China every day. A church is planted in Africa every 24 hours. The number of unreached people groups is slowly shrinking, and even hard-to-crack situations are showing hopeful signs.

How do we take this paradox and discern the role of the church in discipling a nation, or transforming a society? We must, I believe, understand the stages of development of a nation in order to determine the appropriate role of the church in discipling that nation. If we apply the right medicine at the wrong time we can kill the patient. When doing

66   www.barna.org

surgery the physician administers the anesthetic before the surgery, not afterwards; rehabilitative exercise happens after bones are regrown, not before. For too long the church has been a dispensary offering generic vitamins to a world in need of special treatment at different seasons.

I was recently in Nigeria at the time of its 50th anniversary of independence from Britain. I had a sense as I spent the week with friends in government, business and the church that God had a perspective on where they were as a nation. There were many sermons on Jubilee, and much talk about progress, or the lack thereof. When the country gained independence in 1960 it was projected to be one of the leading world nations. They had the assets, the size and the potential. Fifty years later these dreams have not been fulfilled. There are many complex reasons why this is true, and I will leave it to my capable Nigerian friends to analyze their own situation. Contemplating their landmark gave me pause to think about the role of the church in Nigeria, and whether there are truisms that may apply generally in transforming society.

In preparing to speak at a Sunday service celebrating the golden jubilee it struck me that there were distinct phases in national development:

- DEFINING: bringing definition to the geopolitical boundaries of the country. This includes a shift from tribes to nations.

- DISCIPLINING: once a nation is formed, it needs to be disciplined. This sometimes happens with self-discipline, but usually involves a more powerful nation bringing some of its "national sophistication", for want of a better phrase, to bear on the new nation.

- LIBERATING: the nation inevitably goes through a liberation stage where the knowledge-transfer from the disciplining nation has run its course and the locals are ready for self-governance.

- ORDERING: during this phase, the local constitution is formed with an indigenous flavor, and the nation shifts from an externally-imposed law to a rule of law that is a hybrid of local customs and external input. There is agreement on the guiding principles for their new social order.

- SELF-GOVERNANCE: this paves the way for self-governance where the nation matures and functions in an orderly manner, untethered from any mother nation. Without a shift to self-governance the nation will leave too much power in the hands of corporations, be they government, church, not-for-profit or business entities.

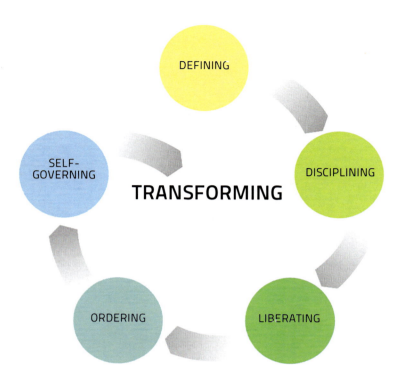

A brief look at the nation of Israel will illustrate these phases.

- DEFINING: The nation began with a man, Abraham, when he responded to God's call. He and his wife produced a son who produced a family that grew into tribes which formed the basis of a nation.
- DISCIPLINING: the family—Jacob and Sons, went into Egypt as a household and came out a nation, but not before they had experienced discipline at the hands of the Egyptians. During their time in Egypt they had good times, and bad times.
- LIBERATING: the story of the exodus from Egypt is well known. Israel had the dramatic and improbable exodus after Moses said, "Let my people go!" (I am sitting next to the Red Sea as I write this, marveling at the passage of a nation across this vast sea... a lot bigger than I remember from the Sunday School stories.) Of course, like every liberation, it was not simply a case of Moses sending Pharaoh a quick email. There were lots of power struggles, flexing of muscles, and reneging on agreements. But liberation came, as it often does.

- ORDERING: while Israel emerged as a nation, they were still a ragtag group that did not have their own national code. The Law was given in the desert, and Israel learned a code of conduct that formed the basis for their economic, religious and social life. This period of ordering took time, as it seems the Israelites were slow to be rid of Egyptian thinking and culture. Crucial to this phase was the introduction of objective truth. God set himself as the foundation for nation-building by weaving a combination of his principles and his presence. Even today, the most sophisticated national code devoid of the person of God will not accomplish the purposes of God.

- SELF-GOVERNANCE: the final stage was the self-governance of a nation guided by the law, the prophets and other godly leaders. Even then, however, scripture anticipated a time when God would write his laws on the hearts of his people, where they would be ruled by the law of the Spirit.

The end goal was the Promised Land, from the perspective of the physical destination. It was never God's end goal, however, as he intended Israel to be a billboard for his goodness and the benefits of his governance. They were to be his poster-child for the presence and principles of the One God on display for all nations.

The cycle can be broken

Unfortunately the cycle of development can be broken. Israel was warned: if you resist the government of God, he will send other nations to redo the Discipline phase. For example, Deuteronomy 4:25-29 says:

> When you beget children and grandchildren and have grown old in the land, and act corruptly and make a carved image in the form of anything, and do evil in the sight of the Lord your God to provoke Him to anger, I call heaven and earth to witness against you this day, that you will soon utterly perish from the land which you cross over the Jordan to possess; you will not prolong your days in it, but will be utterly destroyed. And the Lord will scatter you among the peoples, and you will be left few in number among the nations where the Lord will drive you. And there you will serve gods, the work of men's hands, wood and stone, which neither see nor hear nor eat nor smell. But from there you will seek the Lord your God, and you will find Him if you seek Him with all your heart and with all your soul.

Figure 9: Many nations do not transition from Ordering to Self-Governing. They get sucked, instead, into Lawlessness, and then into chaos. A fresh Disciplining phase inevitably follows.

God anticipated the rebellion of Israel, and cautioned them against forgetting him. The story of the kings is a yo-yo experience of good and bad governance, of fearing God and blatantly defying him. Jerusalem, as of today, has been attacked 37 times! When the nation resisted the order of God and threw off restraint, they were defeated and dispersed until they came to their senses. The cycle of national development can, and often is, broken.

Where does the Church fit into this?

The church can play a key role in calling a nation towards its destiny, or Liberating a nation. Moses thundered—or at least Charlton Heston did—"Let my people go!" Martin Luther King, Jr. said the same thing to a divided America. While Mandela is rightly celebrated in South African history, many church leaders, including the Archbishop Tutu and Dr. Michael Cassidy, to name a few, joined Mandela in challenging the apartheid government to liberate the nation from injustice.

The church can play another key role: Ordering the nation. The Apostle Paul told the Colossians, "yet I am with you in spirit, rejoicing to see your good order and the steadfastness of your faith in Christ."[67] He anticipated order and faith as being hand-in-glove. The book of Deuteronomy is a lexicon of Ordering a nation.

Another way to look at Ordering is through the lens of reconciling all things to Christ, as 2nd Corinthians 5 puts it. There is a danger for the church in this role, however, and this takes us back to the Nigerian story. A simplified view might look like this:

- DEFINING: Many tribes came together and gradually became a people with an identity bigger than any one tribe. While some Nigerians still identify themselves by their tribes, they are, after 50 years, Nigerians. As in many parts of Africa where tribalism is a powerful force, there is still work to do. My friend Dr. Richard Ikiebe commented to me, "After 50 years of independence, Nigeria is still struggling with fudging tribes and ethnic groups into a modern 'nation-state.' For Nigeria, formation into a nation is so fundamental and foundational. The sanctity and the value of a Nigerian life, the responsibilities of government to create and sustain an enabling environment for citizens to pursue their own happiness, the rule of law: these are all areas the nation still needs to be discipled; and who is best equipped to do it than the church?"

- DISCIPLINING: The nation was initially disciplined by Benin (the Lagosians were nice enough to invite them to come and rule), and then the British (who were not invited, but came anyway, expanding various territories to protect economic interests). While the intent of the British was to set up just enough infrastructure to allow them to tap the natural resources of the country, they left behind Nigerians who were more ready to govern themselves.

- LIBERATING: In 1960 the country obtained its independence from Britain. The Union Jack was lowered at midnight on September 30, 1960, and Sir James Wilson Robertson, the top ranking British official, took leave.

- ORDERING: The constitution was defined, and the new government was installed. The country adopted a federal system for its states, and the civil service did a reasonable job for a short while. Things might have gone better had the Brits not sown the seeds for an ongoing national tension: political power was concentrated in the

67   Colossians 2:5 NKJV

hands of a small number of leaders, mostly from the North, and economic power was in the hands of the South. The new Nigeria tried to deal with this reality, but its tribal roots made it a challenge. Order succumbed to lawlessness, and the cycle was broken.

- LAWLESSNESS: the constitution was defied; military rulers stepped into the vacuum, and ruled the country for a cumulative 30 years. (Governed would be too nice a word since they imposed their will, practiced corruption, and did little to build the infrastructure of the nation. It was another form of national Disciplining, now at their own hands.)

- RE-ORDERING: Today Nigeria has returned to democracy, and is experiencing its longest run of liberty. This requires a new round of Ordering—you could call it re-ordering—and it has to run deeper than the constitution. This, in my view, is where the Church in Nigeria has played a pivotal role, namely, creating personal foundations for deepened self-governance.

Most Christians in Nigeria will tell you the church in Nigeria is growing in leaps and bounds. Estimates are that 55% of the national population is Christian. Surely this is aiding the re-ordering and helping the shift from lawlessness. Congregants are first taught to come to church meetings on time, take up a meaningful role in the church family, and be effective family members at home. It cannot stop here. My wife, Lyn, preached in a church in India recently where they announced they were canceling an upcoming Sunday service to go and pick up trash in a local park. Theory inside the church has to translate to action outside the church building. So church goers must be instructed to obey street signs, pick up trash, drive the speed limits, and pay their taxes. A friend from India just returned from a month in Australia. While there he had to learn to drive in obedience to traffic rules; back in India he was unfortunately having to unlearn his new disciplines.

Ordering the church members is not, however, an end in itself. These are the small battles en route to tackling the larger giants of lawlessness and corruption. Church leaders must see themselves as participants in discipling the nation, not as church builders. The same is true in other nations: the Church belongs to Jesus. He builds it so that she can be part of his army mobilized to accomplish his purposes. Pastors are drill sergeants not emperors: they should be training base leaders getting people ready for battle.

Your troops will be willing on your day of battle.[68]

68   Psalm 110:3

It appears, from the limited perspective of an outsider, the churches in Nigeria are at a crossroads. I see three future scenarios for the Church in Nigeria:

- The bigger is better scenario: Churches will see that bigger is better and be enamored with their success in terms of church growth. Large churches will build bigger buildings, and the size of congregations will be the envy of even the Texans. Church busses will give way to church planes as the worldwide Nigerian church franchise grows. Church members will be required to comply with rules and regulations of the church, especially teaching on tithing in order to finance the movement. What was necessary to remedy lawlessness will transition to legalism. When the church becomes legalistic it will lose its "salt and light" quality, and this will result in a decline in the growth.

- The small is everywhere scenario: Churches will see beyond the imposed governance, and pastors will lay hold of their mandate to make people dependent on the leading of the Spirit. Nigerian entrepreneurialism will be reflected in a radical increase in the number of small, more nimble churches. Church leaders will be measured by what they catch, equip and release, rather than what they catch and keep.

- The critical mass to massively critical scenario: Christian leaders will see the sheer size of the church in Nigeria as an asset to steward, and will direct it out toward a needy society in Nigeria, and to the world. The emphasis will shift from an inwardly directed movement to an externally aimed movement. Instead of just having a critical mass of Christians, the focus will be on equipping believers to have a deliberate impact on all facets of society.

In the case of Nigeria, there may well be a combination playing out, most likely the first and third. The challenge for church leaders will be hearing God say "let my people go" when her people are stirred towards the marketplace and other nations. I have used Nigeria as an illustration, but the same is true for any nation where there has been a rapid growth in the church, from the Early Church through today. Take South Korea, for example. It is a miracle story of national transformation due, in large measure, to the rapid influence of the church. A generation later, however, the society has achieved a level of material comfort, and the rate of church growth has begun to decline. Leaders are being challenged to remind their people that the goal was never just a better Korea, but a changed world. Some churches are struggling with succession planning, and the sheer size of the churches has created a magnetic pull that causes an internal focus. Once again God could be saying, "Let my people go!" but this time his audience is not the historic forces of animism, tribalism or nationalism: he is speaking to church leaders. Church leaders need to hear this liberation challenge as a call to channel equipped people towards building the kingdom of God. People quickly tire of building the local church. When they are engaged in the preaching and living of the kingdom of God, they experience the family of God in local churches, and many other expressions, as a by-product of kingdom growth. I am not concerned at all about the demise of the church: it will continue in mega-churches, and house churches, in stadiums and in factories, in churches on the corner in America, and in rice paddies in China. I am, however, concerned about church attendees who are stuck halfway to their true calling. Too many are liberated from the kingdom of darkness, scrubbed-up enough to be respectable church members, but their orderliness has left them neutered when it comes to building the kingdom of God. If you are a pastor, is God whispering, "Let my people go"?

Micro-ordering can have unintended outcomes

Churches can indeed play a key role in the Ordering of a nation. Unless we maintain a rigorous biblical view of the world (and the broader aim of discipling nations) this can have unintended consequences. Kerala is the state in India that has the highest concentration of Christians in the nation. It also has a socialist state government. Local leaders have informed me that the teaching of the church paved the way for communism. The church taught people to be selfless, to share resources, and to respect authority. Its teaching created fertile ground for communist politicians. Ordering just your private world can have unintended consequences if the broader context of reconciling the greater society to Christ is not practiced. Ordering your church without playing a role in Ordering your nation can have the same dulling outcome.

Am I against church growth? Not at all. The rapid rise of a church in a nation, however, has a broader purpose as it can be a:

- Hope-lifter: raising up enough hope-filled people who can see a brighter future touched by the presence, principles and power of God.

- Coalescing community: overcoming the powerlessness that comes through isolation as many followers of God feel they are the only ones in the land. Church growth dispels this myth.

- Training base: not a destination, but a place where people are challenged to work out their destiny by living God-touched lives in untouched places.

- Uniting voice: when a critical mass of Christ-followers unite around God's agenda the Church has a voice in the world, not a just a message for the world. We no longer say, "Come and join us" but "Let us come and serve you."

My historian friend, Dr. Charles Self, tells me, "There is an inverse relationship of institutional control of government and kingdom impact." The rest of this book makes it clear that I am not in favor of Church-controlled politics. The Church has a role, but doing the right thing at the wrong time does not produce the desired outcome. Disciplining when we should be Liberating, Liberating when we should be Ordering, Ordering when we should be weaning people to Self-governance, building our church when we should be establishing the kingdom... all of these can be good activities, but with disastrous outcomes if they are done at the wrong time.

The church can do many right things, but we need the discernment to know our role given the phase of development of the community or nation in which we live. Your context will not be the same as what I have outlined in this chapter. Yours may be a persecuted church, or a minority group, or a stagnating entity no longer appreciative of its historical roots. There is, nonetheless, a role to play: asking questions about the stage of development of your nation will help clarify that role. This will be to God's glory by setting a course of intelligent action.

In this section

Things I think we agree on

Come and let us go

From Mountain to Molehills

Part 7

Call to Action

158   Transforming Society

Things I think we agree on

Most Christ-followers live somewhere between "your kingdom on earth" and "your kingdom one day in heaven." In fact, the majority will not argue with Jesus who instructed us to pray, "Your kingdom come... on earth as it is in heaven." What we differ on is how much, when, and how. The reality is we do not have an option about praying for his kingdom to come. This was an instruction on how and what to pray, not an option. Nevertheless, our understanding of what this "your kingdom come" looks like could place limitations on how much of "your kingdom come" we actually see in practice.

I am not asking you to take a stance at one end of the spectrum or another. Let us get away from the polarized positions and focus on that with which we can agree:

- God is sovereign over all, and he will ultimately accomplish his purposes.
- Everything is his; we belong to him, and he wants us to be part of his purposes.
- He has made provision for us to have the resources we need to get his job done.
- Our primary identity is in God, not a molehill, mountain, country, family, denomination, or career.
- Sectorizing can be useful, but it is not the gospel.
- "Your kingdom come" is both top-down and bottom-up.
- We are God-people not molehill-people, and truth flows from mountains, not hills.
- Assets are distinct from spheres, and we must be stewards of assets at both the personal and societal level. Asset growth and wealth creation are tremendous "nation discipling" tools.
- Households, in their many forms, are key to impacting every sphere of society. This includes the implantation of "church" in households in every sphere of society.
- Signs and wonders—marketplace miracles—are both an effective way for God to market, and an important way for him to reverse the twisting of the DNA of many aspects of society that came through sin.

Some readers may need a little convincing on the last point. I encourage you to look throughout scripture at God's dealings with pre-believers, if you like, and how he regularly invades their world with the supernatural in order to get their attention. Pharaoh is a good example of this. Jesus himself said, "The miracles I do in my Father's name speak for me... I have shown you many great miracles from the Father. For which of these do you stone me?"

My experience today affirms this as we specifically pray for marketplace miracles for businesspeople. When God does miraculously what they cannot explain or do themselves, he gets their attention. They are then far more open to his claim to their domain. Given that we agree on so much, what are we to do? First we need to make a determination to go.

Come and let us go

In Exodus 20 God gave the people of Israel two things: one was a beautiful set of laws that, unfortunately, were impossible for them to keep. The second was an offer for an intimate, supernatural experience of his presence that would at least give them a fear of God and keep them in the zone where they understood the law and were living in the supernatural realm.

> When the people saw the thunder and lightning and heard the trumpet and saw the mountain in smoke, they trembled with fear. They stayed at a distance and said to Moses, "Speak to us yourself and we will listen. But do not have God speak to us or we will die."[69]

Moses understood what was going on and urged them to press into God.

> Do not be afraid. God has come to test you, so that the fear of God will be with you to keep you from sinning.[70]

Instead of saying, "Give us more of your presence or we can never handle these commandments" they said, "We don't want to deal with the spooky stuff that is outside our comfort zone." Yet the manifestation of God's presence is often proportional to the assignment at hand. God does not dish out jobs without offering to be present in whatever way fits the situation, from trumpets to silence. We often run from the smoke and lightning and thunder and trumpets—the things that might be just what we need to carry out the instruction of God.

> The people remained at a distance while Moses approached the thick darkness where God was.[71]

---

69 Exodus 20:18-19
70 Exodus 20:20
71 Exodus 20:21

My main point here is that we can have two reactions to God doing this out of the box thing: one is to step back from the unusual expression of God's presence, and the other is to approach it. I am not specifically equating the mountain of the Lord with unusual experiences, but there is a case for doing so in scripture! What I am saying is that God is calling us to something higher than the "conquering" of molehills. He is calling us to be mountain people... to himself. It requires, for many of us, a decision. "Come and let us go up to the mountain of the Lord."

Let me add one more thing: this Exodus encounter emphasizes that we cannot tackle even a molehill with just laws and principles. We cannot come to the spheres of society with just study and schemes: we desperately need empowering, courage, boldness and equipping that comes from the Spirit. I, for one, will shrink back from my assignment to be a reformer if I am not soaked in the supernatural. The fact that God gives us impossible mandates assures me that he who is faithful will also pour out an inexplicable—outside of Christ—authority to do what is on his heart.

From Mountain to Molehills

How would you answer the question, "What mountain are you from?" I hope that after reading this book you will know that you are from:

- Any mountain

- The mountain of the Lord

- The one mountain where God may have me pitching my tent at present.

If we answer, "I am from Business" or "I am from Healthcare" then we run the risk of making a mountain out of a molehill.

The point is not to establish a new set of "10 molehill conferences"—who would want to buy the tee shirt from a molehill conference? Nor is it to stop the "seven mountain conferences"—there is good truth contained there, and I know many who are being blessed through the insights of wonderful teachers. I do want to appeal, however, to our collective discernment and suggest that we do not enthusiastically charge the next hill without getting the mountain-down perspective.

I also want people to avoid getting pigeon-holed as being from this mountain or that mountain. You are from the mountain of the Lord if you are a son or daughter of the kingdom.

> The field is the world, and the good seed stands for the sons of the kingdom.[72]

He may have you work on any number of mountains at any one time. He may have you live on one mountain for your whole life... but this is unlikely. He might want you to level the mountains, to build them up, or to serve them. He certainly does not want you to deduce that you are from Mountain #1 so you have no jurisdiction over Mountain #4. That is utter nonsense! Let's go back to the words of Abraham Kuijper. "There is not one square inch... about which Jesus Christ does not cry out, 'This is mine!'"

> "Oh, no single piece of our mental world is to be hermetically sealed off from the rest, and there is not a square inch in the whole domain of our human existence over which Christ, who is Sovereign over all, does not cry: 'Mine!'"
>
> *Abraham Kuijper*

In fact, the more likely scenario is what when you get comfortable with your cabin on your molehill God will send you a difficulty to force you to take a trip to another mountain, only to find that the Sovereign Lord reigns there too. When you have made enough trips to enough mountains you will see that they are a subset of a bigger reality, the mountain of the Lord. Pretty soon you will bypass your mastery of this hill or that hill and say, "Come and let us go up to the mountain of the Lord... the chief among the mountains... raised above the hills. He will teach us his ways, so that we may walk in his paths." You will be a top-down, mountain-living, hill-taming, multi-molehill son or daughter of the kingdom.

Prepare the way

John the Baptist was an amazing man with a profound mandate: Prepare the way for the Messiah. He did his job, and Jesus came to a people whose lives were readied for a Redeemer. Jesus is returning; many believe soon. It is now our task to get society—villages, towns, cities, nations—ready for the coming king.

> A voice of one calling in the wilderness,
> "Prepare the way for the Lord, make straight paths for him. Every valley shall be filled in, every mountain and hill made low. The crooked roads shall become straight, the rough ways smooth. And all people will see God's salvation."[73]

72   Matthew 13:38
73   Luke 3:4

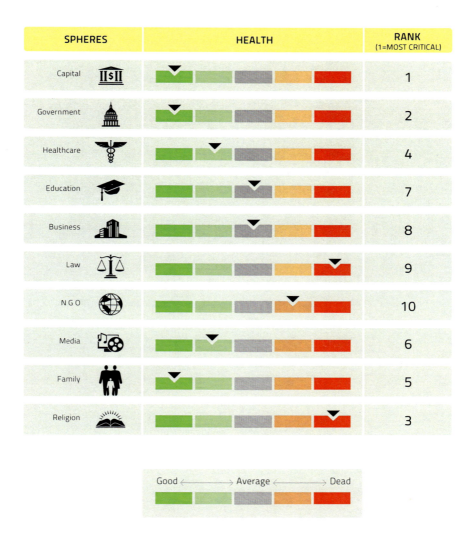

Figure 10: This is another look at The Ten Spheres of Society showing their Health (color coded) and their Ranking (order of importance) in that particular society.

Note how the preparation includes straightening paths: John's advice was practical, covering cheating, generosity and corruption. Preparing the way for Christ's return also includes making every mountain and hill low. As we bring every aspect of life into obedience to the mind of Christ—as we reconcile all facets of life to eternal truth—we prepare the way for Christ's return.

Transforming Society

When William Carey, one my heroes in the faith, attended a minister's fraternal meeting in England he asked a poignant question. The blog, *Missionary Talks*, records it this way:

> *One day William was invited to bring up a topic for the Ministers Fraternal of the Northampton Association and suggested that the churches of England had a responsibility to carry the Gospel to the nations of the world. This was not at all a popular view in 1787. The belief at the time was that it was the responsibility of the Apostles to share the Gospel. When they died, the job did too!*

There is a popular story in the life of William Carey, which came out of this meeting, though there are questions as to its accuracy. It is said that as William was making his case for the need of churches to evangelize the heathen that the father of his friend John Ryland stood up and said: "If God wanted the heathen to know, He would tell them Himself without any help from man." Whether John Ryland, Sr. said these words or not, it was obvious to those involved that this was the popular view at the time.

I am not sure I know a follower of Jesus today who is serious about their faith who would argue with what we generally call "The Great Commission." For decades many have so faithfully taught on the need to "make disciples of all nations" that we now believe it is possible. Coupled with a serious prospect of revival, thinking about domains produces the possibility-thinking about societal transformation that is becoming pervasive today. While the general population is becoming pessimistic about the future, kingdom-minded Christians are becoming more optimistic. We are seeing and believing that people in the mainstream of all spheres of society are starting to look to men and women of faith for solutions to large scale problems. Often these ambassadors of a new future operate without a formal church label—Bono and the Red Campaign being but one example—and speak in non-religious terms. The kingdom of God is expanding daily and, even in the Muslim world, great advances are being made. The estimate is that 30,000 believers are baptized every day in China.

The idea of spheres can help focus the task. If we take a wrong view of domains, however, we will simply produce a crop of newly dichotomized disciples. To reiterate, it is a serious concern to meet zealous people who are constricted because they feel they do not know which mountain they are from. The consequences of bad theology are bad, even when they are unintended. If, however, we are armed with a biblical worldview for all spheres of society, then we can live out our mandate in every aspect of life. If we harbor vestiges of the secular-sacred divide, however, we will quickly try to tame wild initiatives in any sphere and make them part of "church." This tragedy would spring from our sinful tendency to control rather than our biblical charter to bring freedom. Of course we would not be so bald-faced as to say we are trying to control a movement, but we will add labels about apostolic-this and accountability-that... and neuter marketplace ministers before they leave the church lobby.

Our job as apostles, prophets, evangelists and pastor-teachers is to equip people for the work of the ministry. People from the sphere of Religion are not necessarily the best equipped to do this for people in the other spheres, although they do have a significant role to play. I am so encouraged by the fact that churches and universities are thinking more intentionally about the spheres. At the same time, we need to remember that the end game is transforming society—in Christ's words, making disciples of all nations—and not simply adding layers of lingo to people already burdened with over-categorization. Stated another way, societal transformation is not about the Religion sector shaping the others, but about Repurposing Religion so that it shifts from church to kingdom while we simultaneously repurpose all spheres of society with the common goal of transforming society.

When we look to the back of God's book, we see this tremendous statement about the future in which we are to participate.

> Then the seventh angel sounded; and there were loud voices in heaven, saying, "The kingdom of the world has become the kingdom of our Lord and of His Christ; and He will reign forever and ever."
>
> And the twenty-four elders, who sit on their thrones before God, fell on their faces and worshipped God, saying, "We give You thanks, O Lord God, the Almighty, who are and who were, because You have taken Your great power and have begun to reign."[74]

I, for one, am looking forward to seeing this. Like you, I also want to do what I can to see the rightful reign of King Jesus extended through the Spirit to every sphere of society today. He shall reign forever and ever, and he has started that reign in you and in me right here, right now.

Hallelujah!

74 Revelation 11:15-17

166 Transforming Society

A Call to Action

In this section

Transformational Tools

End Note #1 Public Private Partnership

End Note #2 PPP Examples

Index

About the Author

Other books by the Author

Appendices

170 Transforming Society

Transformational Tools

Repurposing Business

The challenge of making a difference through one's work doesn't stem from lack of knowledge, desire or even lack of empowerment. In working with hundreds of businesses and business leaders worldwide, we know that true impact is realized when you:

- Maximize every activity to serve and improve the lives of those around you,
- Leverage your unique strengths and assets to tackle societal ills and,
- Align and engage those in your sphere of influence around a greater purpose.

If it's your desire to be a catalyst for meaningful and lasting change in society, take the next step in Repurposing Business. www.inst.net has more details.

Kingdom Business Assessment

It is common for people to say, "I am a businessperson and a Christian, therefore I run a 'Christian business', whatever that is." This false assumption—I am Christian so my business is serving God's purpose—led us to develop a short Kingdom Business Assessment that will provoke discussion about just how kingdom the business really is.

Kingdom Impact Assessment

It would be good if every church were building the kingdom of God. Often the issue is not desire, but know-how, so we have developed a Kingdom Impact Assessment that enables church leaders to self-reflect on how much their organization, programs and wineskin is actually creating a kingdom impact.

Societal Impact Assessment

Corporations are measured more and more by the Impact that they have on their constituents, local and global. Whether it is "the triple bottom line" or an analysis of corporate social responsibility, the trend is towards meaningful coexistence.

At The Institute we help corporations go beyond a defensive posture towards a deliberate and positive strategy of playing a leading role in societal transformation, on Purpose. There are certain things that Business can do that governments cannot do alone. There are corporate strategies that are good for the company, and good for society; good for today, and good for eternity.

Asset Evaluation

Rather than focus on just the needs and issues in a society, one can use any of a number of approaches to determining the assets of a community. The Asset Based Community Development (ABCD)[75] approach is one, and Asset Mapping another.[76] At The Institute we have analyzed assets and needs using The 10-F Model® and then looked first at what businesses could be started to address societal gaps. There are definitely other issues which need to be addressed be social sector organizations, churches and families.

75   http://www.synergos.org/knowledge/02/abcdoverview.htm
76   Mapping the Assets of your Community: A Key component for building local capacity, by Lionel J. Beaulieu, Southern Rural Development Center

Public Private Partnerships

Endnote # 1

A quick Google search will unearth lots on the topic. For example, Wikipedia.org defines PPP as follows.

Public-private partnership (PPP) describes a government service or private business venture which is funded and operated through a partnership of government and one or more private sector companies. These schemes are sometimes referred to as PPP, P3 or P3.

PPP involves a contract between a public sector authority and a private party, in which the private party provides a public service or project and assumes substantial financial, technical and operational risk in the project. In some types of PPP, the cost of using the service is borne exclusively by the users of the service and not by the taxpayer. In other types (notably the private finance initiative), capital investment is made by the private sector on the strength of a contract with government to provide agreed services and the cost of providing the service is borne wholly or in part by the government. Government contributions to a PPP may also be in kind (notably the transfer of existing assets). In projects that are aimed at creating public goods like in the infrastructure sector, the government may provide a capital subsidy in the form of a one-time grant, so as to make it more attractive to the private investors. In some other cases, the government may support the project by providing revenue subsidies, including tax breaks or by providing guaranteed annual revenues for a fixed period.

Typically, a private sector consortium forms a special company called a "special purpose vehicle" (SPV) to develop, build, maintain and operate the asset for the contracted period. In cases where the government has invested in the project, it is typically (but not always) allotted an equity share in the SPV. The consortium is usually made up of a building contractor, a maintenance company and bank lenders). It is the SPV that signs the contract with the government and with subcontractors to build the facility and then maintain it. In the infrastructure sector, complex arrangements and contracts that guarantee and secure the cash flows, make PPP projects prime candidates for Project financing. A typical PPP example would be a hospital building financed and constructed by a private developer and then leased to the hospital authority. The private developer then acts as landlord, providing housekeeping and other non-medical services while the hospital itself provides medical services.

PPP Examples

Endnote # 2

Source:
Canadian Council for Public-Private Partnerships,
http://www.pppcouncil.ca/aboutPPP_definition.asp

- Operation & Maintenance Contract (O & M): A private operator, under contract, operates a publicly-owned asset for a specified term. Ownership of the asset remains with the public entity.

- Design-Build-Finance-Operate (DBFO): The private sector designs, finances and constructs a new facility under a long-term lease, and operates the facility during the term of the lease. The private partner transfers the new facility to the public sector at the end of the lease term.

- Build-Own-Operate (BOO): The private sector finances, builds, owns and operates a facility or service in perpetuity. The public constraints are stated in the original agreement and through on-going regulatory authority.

- Build-Own-Operate-Transfer (BOOT): A private entity receives a franchise to finance, design, build and operate a facility (and to charge user fees) for a specified period, after which ownership is transferred back to the public sector.

- Buy-Build-Operate (BBO): Transfer of a public asset to a private or quasi-public entity usually under contract that the assets are to be upgraded and operated for a specified period of time. Public control is exercised through the contract at the time of transfer.

- Operation License: A private operator receives a license or rights to operate a public service, usually for a specified term. This is often used in IT projects.

- Finance Only: A private entity, usually a financial services company, funds a project directly or uses various mechanisms such as a long-term lease or bond issue.

Index

A

Adams, John Quincy—79
Adams, Samuel—79
Asset Evaluation—170
Assets—8, 14, 15, 50, 58, 61, 62, 63,
    80, 102, 105, 108, 127, 133, 144,
    157, 170, 171, 172

B

B Corporations—101
BELTS—88, 97, 98
Boyd, Gregory—31
    Boyd—31, 32, 33
Bright, Bill—11, 24
Business as Missions—18, 49, 51,
    54, 55, 92, 95
    BAM—54, 93

C

Call2All—93
Called Corporations—88, 106, 107
    Called Corporation—106
Calvin, John—22
    Calvin—22, 116
Caperna, Al—93
Capital—44, 46, 49, 50, 51, 66, 67,
    78, 87, 93, 104, 105, 107, 118, 179
Carey, William—162
Cassidy, Michael—85, 147
Christian—10, 22, 23, 24, 26, 29, 31,
    32, 40, 55, 76, 79, 81, 85, 91, 106,
    108, 115, 122, 125, 130, 137, 149,
    150, 169
Christianity Today—31, 33
Communist Manifesto—23
competencies—86, 92, 99, 104, 108
Constantinian—33
Constitution—79, 148
Convergence—34, 40, 179
Cope, Landa—11, 25, 93
cosmos—32, 77, 109
Cunningham, Loren—11, 24, 116

D

Declaration of Independence—79
defeatism—16, 18, 32
dichotomy—13, 33, 43, 177
domain—13, 14, 23, 25, 26, 43, 49,
    52, 53, 56, 158. *See also* Sphere
    domains—11, 13, 15, 25, 27, 30,
        33, 34, 43, 162
Domainationalism—18, 33
dominionism—16, 18, 29, 32, 79

E

Education—25, 28, 37, 40, 43, 50, 52, 61, 62, 66, 67, 82, 84, 85, 87, 127, 128
  education—23, 25, 40, 43, 51, 52, 62, 81, 84, 85, 97, 100, 105, 122, 127, 128
Eldred, Ken—93
Enlow, Johnny—26, 28
ethnos—22, 47, 77

F

Family—25, 40, 45, 52, 66, 67, 82, 83, 123, 124, 134
foundations—10, 14, 72, 73, 74, 86, 129, 149
Foundations of a City—70, 73. *See also* Foundations

G

Gauteng—73
Globalization—48. *See also* global
glory of God—16, 76, 77, 92, 99, 106, 109, 114, 115, 116, 117, 118, 121, 122, 128, 130, 134, 136. *See also* glory
Government—25, 30, 37, 40, 43, 52, 56, 64, 66, 67, 79, 80, 82, 84, 104, 105, 118, 120, 137, 171
Guinness—47, 81, 106
  Guinness, Os—81

H

Healthcare—44, 52, 66, 67, 84, 104, 126, 127, 159
  healthcare—27, 44, 51, 52, 62, 84, 105, 127
Hillman, Os—24, 26, 93
Households—45, 88, 94, 99, 100, 157

I

ICCC—93
Inside Work—93
I-Operations—51, 75, 130, 179

J

Johnson, Bill—26, 93
Judiciary
  Judicial—79

K

key performance indicators
  KPI—74, 116
Kuijper, Abraham
  Kuijper—11, 13, 23, 53, 82, 160
  Kuyper—11, 13, 23, 160
Kvamme, Mark—91

L

Law—37, 40, 44, 46, 49, 52, 62, 63, 65, 80, 81, 105, 121, 137, 145
Lewis, C.S.—22
Local Agency Formation
  Commissions—25
  LAFCO—25

M

molehills
  molehill—13, 18, 26, 28, 37, 38, 40, 41, 51, 54, 63, 70, 74, 76, 114, 159
Mouw, Richard—31
Muslim—91, 162

N

Naugle, David K—22
NGOs—45, 46, 49, 52, 65, 66, 67, 81, 82, 84, 102, 107, 122, 177
   NGO—65, 67, 81
Nigeria—144, 148, 149, 150
Nordstrom, Dwight—93

O

Olson, Gunnar—93
Orr, James—22
   Orr—22, 23
Otis, George Jr—93, 116
Oxford University—85

P

parachurch—18, 55, 56
Peacocke, Dennis—93
Petrie, Alistair—11, 25, 73, 93
Pew Forum—79
pluralism—24
Power, Graham—9, 93
Public Private Partnerships
   PPP—63, 171

R

Redding—9, 14, 96
reformation—64, 92, 121
Religion—37, 45, 50, 52, 54, 56, 66, 67, 82, 86, 96, 128, 129, 163
rēp—2, 69, 73, 75, 93, 100, 104, 137
Repurposing Business—2, 78, 88, 104, 107, 108, 109, 169
Repurposing Capital—18, 49, 58, 70, 78, 179
Revelation—9, 15, 40, 41, 46, 47, 53, 86, 104, 117, 127, 128
Roberts, Bob—25
Rose, Charlie—31, 32
Rwanda—30
Ryland, John—162

S

Schaeffer, Francis—23, 24
   Schaeffer—23, 24, 53
sector—28, 33, 37, 40, 41, 49, 51, 53, 54, 56, 66, 67, 74, 75, 76, 77, 79, 80, 81, 82, 83, 84, 85, 102, 105, 116, 121, 127, 163, 170, 171, 172, 177.
   See also Sphere
secular humanism—24
Self, Charles—151
Seven Mountains
   7Mountain—13
   seven mind molders—13
Sider, Ron—31
Signs and Wonders—98
Silvoso, Ed—25, 93
Smith, James K.A.—31
   Smith—31, 33
Sphere
   sphere—9, 11, 13, 14, 15, 16, 23, 25, 27, 28, 29, 30, 33, 38, 39, 40, 41, 43, 47, 49, 50, 51, 52, 53, 54, 55, 56, 57, 61, 62, 65, 74, 75, 76, 77, 78, 82, 96, 98, 104, 105, 106, 113, 116, 117, 118, 120, 121, 122, 123, 124, 125, 126, 127, 128, 129, 130, 137, 157, 163
   sphere sovereignty—13, 23, 29, 82

T

The 10-F Model
   The 10-Fs—130
The 10-P Model
   The 10-Ps—130
The Institute—2, 13, 51, 64, 69, 76, 92, 93, 99, 101, 102, 104, 107, 130, 169, 170, 177
The Mountain of the Lord—11, 18, 21, 34, 57
theocracy—23
Theology—10, 85

theonomy—29
Transforming Society—9, 11, 60, 88, 103, 162

V
Vallaton, Kris—14

W
Wallis, Jim—31
wineskin—47, 74, 85, 86, 130, 169
worldview—11, 22, 84, 85, 107, 108, 127, 162

Z
Zaccharais, Ravi—25

Symbols
7Mountain. *See also* Seven Mountains

About the Author

Brett Johnson founded **The Institute for Innovation, Integration & Impact, Inc**. in 1996. His writings complement the work of this Silicon Valley think tank. Brett has over thirty years experience with leading public accounting and management consulting firms, helping corporations from global multi-nationals through to business start-ups and social sector organizations. Brett was a Partner at KPMG Peat Marwick and at Computer Sciences Corporation. He spent fourteen years at Price Waterhouse working in South Africa in the United States. He is passionate about the abolition of dichotomy—eradicating the false barriers between facets of life, especially the so-called secular and sacred.

Brett and the team at The Institute have repurposed hundreds of corporations, working extensively with executive teams helping them envision new futures, and aligning such teams around a common purpose. These include businesses, NGOs and international charities. The team at The Institute has developed intellectual property and frameworks to rapidly analyze corporations and help them discover a fresh purpose that radically increases their focus, alignment and impact.

Brett is a Chartered Accountant and holds a Bachelor's degree in Commerce from the University of Cape Town. He lives in Silicon Valley with his wife, Lyn. They have four grown children: Fay, James and his wife, Jessica; and Davey.

Brett Johnson is frequently asked to speak and conduct consultations for leaders and corporations. For more information on Brett Johnson and the products and services offered by The Institute for Innovation, Integration & Impact, Inc. please contact us. We look forward to hearing from you!

Contact Information

 info@inst.net

 1-866-9INDABA

 www.inst.net

E-books (including Kindle) are also available.

Other Books by the Author

Convergence—*Integrating your Career, Community, Creativity and Calling (2000, 2010)*

I-Operations: the Impact of the Internet on Operating Models with Gary Daichendt, the former EVP of Worldwide Operations at Cisco (2000). The second edition is titled I-Operations: How the Internet can transform your Operating Model (2003).

LEMON Leadership®—Radically fresh leadership (2005, 2010)

Repurposing Capital (2010)—Rediscovering Faith-based Financing

CYCLES: A journey to Purpose (2010)

He has also authored numerous papers and articles.